Go
START
SOMETHING

Go
START
SOMETHING

LIVE LIFE ON THE EDGE

50 Rules
for the entrepreneur

BY JAN COLLMER

iUniverse, Inc.
Bloomington

GO START SOMETHING
Live Life on the Edge

iUniverse books may be ordered through booksellers or by contacting:

iUniverse
1663 Liberty Drive
Bloomington, IN 47403
www.iuniverse.com
1-800-Authors (1-800-288-4677)

ISBN: 978-1-4697-6368-2 (sc)
ISBN: 978-1-4697-6369-9 (hc)
ISBN: 978-1-4697-6390-3 (ebk)

Library of Congress Control Number: 2012901662

Printed in the United States of America

iUniverse rev. date: 06/19/2012

TABLE OF CONTENTS

Foreword vii
Introduction xiii
Jan's **50 rules** for the entrepreneur xxiii
    The 12 most important **rules** xxiii
    12 good habits necessary for **starting** a business xxvi
    7 Cautionary **rules** xxviii
    19 Leadership **rules** xxx

1.   Great Entrepreneurs 1
2.   My Early Years 9
3.   Starting Something 18
4.   No Partnerships! 33
5.   Goal setting 38
6.   Save 10% 50
7.   Luck 62
8.   Mentors 68
9.   The law of unintended consequences 73
10. Delegation 77
11. Inclusion and recognition 83
12. Decision-making 91
13. Cash flow 96
14. Control! 102
15. Calendar freedom and time for play 106
16. Contracts 114
17. Pricing 119
18. Conclusion 124

Acknowledgments 127

FOREWORD

Jan Collmer has been a good friend for nearly twenty years. I've had the privilege of working with him in a variety of roles—both personal and professional—and I consider him one of the wisest, most straightforward and generous individuals I've ever known. Although we've shared a lot over the past two decades—including a love of aviation, a close association with the US Navy, and a fascination with entrepreneurship—we don't necessarily agree on everything. Over the years, we've had some spirited intellectual debates over politics, economics, religion, and the challenges of everyday life.

I was delighted when Jan asked me to write a foreword for this book—he had asked me to read an earlier draft and give him my thoughts.

I'm not quite sure why Jan picked me—but perhaps he figured that a few words from a professor of entrepreneurship might lend a bit of gravitas and academic credibility to his authorship. I'm more of a practitioner than an academic, however, with more than thirty years of "real world" experience before earning a PhD and embarking on a teaching career in my mid-fifties. Although the wisdom he imparts in the pages that follow would be valuable to students as well as aspiring entrepreneurs, Jan's message speaks to me more directly in the context of my experience as an entrepreneur and businessman.

Let me explain. I got into academia through the back door. After about ten years as a finance and marketing officer in Fortune 200 companies in the '70s, I shepherded two companies through the IPO process and managed several turnarounds as a CFO or COO in the '80s. By the late 1980s I was running a successful turnaround management consulting practice. Sometimes, however, life has a way of taking you where you didn't expect to go. In 1990, in a casual conversation with the Dean of the business school at UT Arlington, I admitted that I had once considered following my father's footsteps in an academic career. The Dean baited his hook, dared me to enroll in the PhD program in his school, and eventually reeled me in. I earned my degree in 1995 and taught at Southern Methodist University for several years before I joined the UT Dallas faculty in 2001.

In the course of my doctoral studies, I was intrigued by Peter Drucker's *Innovation and Entrepreneurship*, written in 1985. A couple of passages still resonate with me:

> *Entrepreneurship is "risky" mainly because so few of the so-called entrepreneurs know what they are doing. They lack the methodology. They violate elementary and well-known rules.*

> *Unless a new venture develops into a new business and makes sure of being "managed," it will not survive no matter how brilliant the entrepreneurial idea, no matter how much money it attracts, no matter how good its products, nor even how great the demand for them.*

Go Start Something!!! This book provides a rich and overflowing treasure chest of useful advice for any small businessman or would-be entrepreneur. Jan's practical suggestions are right on target! I've watched him in action for years, and this is real, learned-from-experience advice. Jan has practiced what he preaches. Over my career, I've encountered many situations similar to those described in the pages that follow—a number of which might have been handled more effectively had I had this book in my hands at the time.

At UT Dallas, I teach an MBA class in leadership. In my opening lecture in the first class of the semester, I tell my students:

> *When I got my MBA forty-five years ago, there were no courses in leadership. So everything I'm going to teach you, I learned along the way by "screwing up"!*

I hope that that statement is not literally true—I've had some successes along the way—but it always gets a good laugh and reinforces the point that experience is frequently the best teacher. That's why this book can be so valuable—both to experienced and practicing entrepreneurs, and to aspiring beginners just starting out on their own adventure of a lifetime.

For the beginner, this book can be an invaluable road map—helping them to avoid tripping over the "elementary and well-known rules" that Peter Drucker described. For the experienced entrepreneur, it can serve as a useful reminder and checklist of important concepts and practices, perhaps once learned, but occasionally forgotten or ignored in the heat of battle.

Along the way as you read, and may often reread, the chapters of this book, you'll get a sense of Jan Collmer the man—and a remarkable man he is. Among his many interests, Jan has been a great supporter of the Jesuit College Preparatory School in Dallas. There is probably no better three-word summation of Jan Collmer than the school's motto "*Men for Others.*" I have watched Jan walking through his company's factory or in the employee lunchroom, stopping to chat with the workers, remembering their names, and demonstrating an abiding concern and caring for each.

He has given freely of his time and financial resources to dozens of civic groups and charitable causes, and been an active supporter of the educational programs of a number of local universities.

Throughout this book, Jan makes a big deal about maintaining control and avoiding partnerships, but Jan consistently treated his employees, customers and suppliers as if they were partners—in the best sense of the word. Jan's employees and business associates have returned the favor with exceptional loyalty. ***Leadership rule 5*** states: ***"Fairness in all your dealings will serve you well in business and at home."*** Honesty, integrity and fairness are a big deal to Jan—far more important than money, as the following story will illustrate.

Several years ago, Jan asked me to help him by negotiating and managing the sale of one of his companies to a prospective buyer, who also happened to be a competitor. Jan was concerned that the buyer might terminate some of the employees and asked me to include a clause in the purchase agreement that required the buyer, in the event any of the employees were terminated within the first several months after the sale, to abide by the generous severance arrangements that Jan had always provided to his employees. Within a month after the sale, the buyer terminated several of the employees without living up to the severance agreement. Within hours after hearing of this, Jan called me and asked me to calculate the difference between the two weeks' severance the employees had been paid and what they would have been paid under the former policy. He then made up the difference out of his own pocket. "Fair is fair," he told me, "and these people have been fair to me—I could do no less." That is a lesson that adds an exclamation point to ***Leadership Rule 5***.

In ***Leadership Rule 3*** Jan advises the aspiring entrepreneur to ***"maintain a sense of humor."*** He lives by this rule, too, although occasionally his sense of humor is appreciated only in retrospect.

In Chapter 2, Jan briefly mentions one of his hobbies—that of an acrobatic "stunt pilot" performing at airshows around the country. Jan took me along for a ride as he practiced his airshow routine several years ago. It was a cold January day and I was wearing a bulky leather jacket. Before we took off, he asked me if my shoulder straps were tight. I assured him that they were. As we flew out to the practice area, he repeated his question and I again responded in the affirmative. I suspect he knew otherwise, but rather than debate the point with me, he suddenly flipped the aircraft, an Extra 300L on its back. There I was, upside down, hanging in the shoulder straps, with several inches of clearance between the seat and my backside. After letting me hang there for ten or fifteen seconds, he rolled the Extra back to level flight and I cinched myself in tightly. We had a good laugh over that.

Since that occasion, Jan has generously provided all three of my sons, each now a pilot, and a son-in-law with memorable rides in the Extra as he practiced his routines. Not for the faint of heart or anyone with a fear of heights, but great fun, nonetheless.

Leadership Rule 17 advises *"don't take yourself too seriously,"* and Jan lives by that rule as well. We are *both members of a group of twelve that meets twice a month for dinner and discussion.* Throughout 1999, Jan was convinced that the Y2K computer glitch would wreak havoc on our ability to do business as usual, including speculation about rioting in the streets as the government was brought to its knees by computer failures. I took the opposite view—it was a technical problem, with a date certain, and adequate time to implement the necessary "fixes" before the calendar rolled into the next century. We had a spirited debate that extended over many months. As it turns out, Y2K was a non-event. In the first meeting of January 2000, Jan hosted the meeting of the group and celebrated the occasion with a cake, decorated with the image of a black crow, so that he could publicly "eat crow" over the Y2K issue.

Aviator, successful entrepreneur, businessman, civic leader, mentor, and a generous friend to many . . . and now an author, to boot! It's an easy read, but take it in small doses and let the lessons sink in. There is a lifetime of wisdom in these pages. Thanks, Jan, for sharing it with all of us.

Joseph C. Picken, Ph.D.
Executive Director
The Institute for Innovation and Entrepreneurship at UT Dallas

INTRODUCTION

Why should I *go start something*? Why take all the risk to start something when a stable, well-paying job will do? Why go start something with all the attendant stress and worries and the probable 80-hour work weeks?

Those questions are important and deserve reasonable answers. I will try to give you a few of the answers along with some business ideas, ideas that are universal in any kind of business start-up. What I will *not* give you are ideas for the kind of business you should start or sources of financing other than very general guidelines. Those are ideas for another book.

I will share with you my list of *Rules for the Entrepreneur.* None of these *rules* are absolutes but you should at least consider them before you venture off into the entrepreneurial world. My *rules* spring from observations that I have accumulated over a long career of relatively successful, medium-scale entrepreneurial activity. Think of the *rules* as a checklist and use it in that way. I think you will profit personally if you at least briefly consider each of the points that are set out before you try to start a business.

You might be interested in the development of my list of *rules* for the entrepreneur. Over the last 20 years I have had the pleasure of being a guest lecturer at several of the graduate management schools in the Dallas/Fort Worth area. Over that period of time I have collected and developed a large sheaf of lecture notes to help me in my presentations. A few years ago, a management consultant friend, John Dealey, sent me a small business-sized card in the mail that had his 10 rules for management on it. I studied those rules and concluded that if they were for a very large, bureaucratic corporation they would make complete sense. On the other hand, in my opinion, my relatively small entrepreneurial company and any other entrepreneurial enterprise would have little use for those particular rules.

So, I decided that I would write the 10 management **rules for the entrepreneur**. My list of **rules** grew quite lengthy and was primarily derived from my collection of lecture notes. Several of the professors whose classes I visited suggested that I consider writing a book that dealt with some of the issues and examples contained in my classroom discussion of the **rules**. So for the purposes of this book, I've consolidated the **rules** into a shorter collection of chapters in this book.

I certainly haven't had anything like the spectacularly successful careers of Bill Gates, Michael Dell or a relatively small group of other amazing entrepreneurs … and few of us ever will. All of us can, and probably should, admire or maybe even envy these incredible men, their meteoric careers and the fabulous wealth they have accumulated. We can easily see and appreciate these pioneers and all the other high flying entrepreneurs whose tremendous service to our free enterprise system has provided unique benefits to all of us who use computers and the many other advanced products and services we now take for granted.

Most of us are unlikely to equal or exceed these ultra-entrepreneurs' performance. Nor are we likely to match the great financial masters such as Donald Trump, John Templeton or Warren Buffett. On the other hand, my own business life and that of many entrepreneurial friends can be considered reasonable successes and we accumulated significant wealth in the process.

And you can too. So go ahead, "make my day" … **go start something**!

If you decide to be a beginning entrepreneur, I want to help you succeed, not necessarily on the superstar scale, but on a personally satisfying scale, whether large or small. You may be able to succeed in the great American free enterprise system along with the huge number of lesser players who have scored well in the pursuit of progress, wealth and personal independence by starting their own businesses. One thing for sure: you will be moving well out of your comfort zone!

The purpose of this book is not to give advice to the advanced entrepreneur, although he or she might find it interesting. Rather my intention is to help guide the raw beginner through the thought and decision processes necessary for the entrepreneurial wanna-be, you, the first time start-up entrepreneur. I want to help you see and avoid some of the many traps that can lead to personal grief and potential financial failure. If I save you just one headache, my work will be justified!

It is not my mission to deal with major entrepreneurial efforts on the scale of several millions or billions of dollars in capitalizations. The entrepreneur that I intend to talk to is the great class of beginning entrepreneurs who can succeed at something less than mega-ventures. If you look around a large city (I live in Dallas, Texas), you will see thousands of large homes, McMansions. Who owns these beautiful homes? There are lots of sources of personal wealth: inheritance; rich spouse; career success in a large corporation. But most of these homes are owned by successful entrepreneurs. Some owners are small-business operators and some are large-business managers, many of whom actually started their own businesses.

If you are both very lucky **and** smart, you may break away from the working crowd and go into orbit with a mega-success as an entrepreneur. You certainly won't if you don't try! There should be no limit to one's dreams; most successes begin with an impossible dream. Be warned: Pessimists rarely accomplish anything worthwhile!

There are hundreds of thousands of small entrepreneurial businesses in the United States and many business opportunities remain that can be grown into sizeable companies with a bit of effort and luck. You, the emerging entrepreneur, are the one I would like to help and hopefully I can provide you with information you consider useful.

To repeat, my goal is not to determine what kind of business you should start or where you should seek capital, or what markets you should try to enter; rather, this book is intended to provide a checklist that will give you a base from which to consider any opportunity and to consider in advance the multiple problems that you will face before you begin to move forward into the entrepreneurial world.

We go back to the *rules*. The *rules* are not immutable; they are just checkpoints in your decision process. Any one rule, or a majority of the *rules*, may be violated and not upset the success of your project. But, you should at least consider all the *rules* as a checklist before you head off into the jungle of entrepreneurial business start-ups. Many entrepreneurial enterprises have hit the rocks due to failure to observe one or another of these *rules*. The *rules* are drawn from my experience and observation for over a period of fifty years.

As the Boy Scouts say, be prepared! The best way to be prepared is to review the rules.

Consideration of the *rules* will help you detect some of the explosive land mines that lay in wait for your misstep. Be at least forewarned that there are traps out there. To be forewarned is to be forearmed. Bad judgment is one issue and negligence is another. You may be guilty of bad judgment from time to time but you should avoid negligence like the plague.

Sadly, it may be impossible for me to help if you fail to carefully consider these rules before you start a venture. Most critical mistakes are made at the very beginning of a new business. Solving these issues later can cause a lot of unnecessary pain and grief. So read the rules first.

The *rules* checklist is the take-home value of this book!

If you have a somewhat innovative mindset and are an active, hard-working person and interested in controlling your own fate, the entrepreneurial world may be for you. Now you may have a hint as to the *"why"* you should *go start something*.

The only, I repeat, the only, path to wealth, significant wealth, other than a good inheritance, a rich spouse, or an improbable career move to the top of a Fortune 1000 company is to own and operate your own business. The best way to own and operate a business is to start one, so *go start something!*

Dream, dare, and do!!!

The monetary rewards of entrepreneurship are certainly important, and profitability is essential to business growth, but the personal satisfaction and self-esteem gained in the process are more rewarding and are almost impossible to achieve any other way. The independence of owning your own business is absolutely golden. It is the most powerful feeling in the world to have almost absolute control of your own future and your own calendar. No "job-job" can ever match the feeling of freedom you will get from making your own decisions as to use of your time and resources.

Even if wealth is not your primary motivation, personal freedom and independence are reasons enough to make the choice for a personally-owned, entrepreneurial business. All of this is not to say the path to personal ownership is always short or easy, but a favorable outcome, a profitable self-owned business, is worth whatever effort it takes to get there.

Calendar freedom, more than money, may actually be the greatest reward for the successful entrepreneur.

On the other hand, the easiest path in the business world is to stay out of a start-up entrepreneurial business. I have no problem with someone who finds a good job and sticks with it and retires with full benefits. For most people that will be the answer to their life goals. But, those who never try to start something are missing out on the adventure of a lifetime.

It is not necessary to start a business from scratch, although I personally consider a start-up venture to be the most exciting and satisfying approach. Small—to medium-size operating businesses can be acquired. Businesses are available for purchase more or less continuously. Owners sell for a variety of reasons: health, retirement, marital issues, etc. A brief Internet search will result in the names of numerous business brokers in your local area. Careful research and your own good negotiating skills can yield an excellent result. But be careful; unfortunately, there are a few bad actors in the business broker world.

Great care is required in analyzing and understanding the actual financial condition of a possible acquisition, its history with its suppliers and its customers. The risks of the unknown and largely unknowable past history of a small business and the difficult task of proper financial evaluation may leave you with a king-sized headache or, even worse, a financial disaster, in record time. Work the financial data carefully. Over-paying for a business makes an already tough job even tougher.

If you decide to move forward and pursue acquisition of an existing business, you must discover why the present owners are selling it. Admittedly, there are usually good answers to that question such as those mentioned above: old age, disability or divorce. But, you need to investigate and clearly understand the owner's motives and be on the lookout for purposely hidden weaknesses. You don't want to unknowingly buy into other people's problems. The services of a really good accountant and a seasoned lawyer are indispensable to a good acquisition.

If you have some personal insight into the target business and the markets that it serves, that might eliminate some of the mystery and may somewhat mitigate your risk. Nevertheless, you simply cannot be too careful in an acquisition. The owner and the business broker will spin a favorable tale regardless of the facts. Picture a used car salesman!

Every dollar and every hour you spend on due diligence will be rewarded. You must not be afraid to pry into every detail of the target company's sales history, accounts receivable, accounts payable, inventory, stability of the customer base, credit ratings, hidden liabilities and most importantly, the status of key employees. For many businesses, especially sales-oriented businesses, the employees are the primary assets and are the key to future success. They walk out every evening at 5 PM and might not come back if they decide you are the wrong owner. This will test your human relations skill! You must assure yourself of the continued availability of key employees. Every item on the balance sheet must be checked out in detail. As the old saying has it: "The devil is in the details!"

And don't forget the most important rule when it comes to an acquisition: *"caveat emptor,"* let the buyer beware!

A big risk in any acquisition is the possibility, even the probability, that the company has dead inventory (assuming there is inventory involved). Inventories go stale for a number of reasons: obsolescence or spoilage, particularly for organic items and chemicals, breakage, corrosion in metal products, water damage from leaky roofs, pests and insect damage, or even misstatements of facts. The list of possibilities is long. Don't expect the seller to point out these inventory deficiencies. That's your job as you or your agents do due-diligence inspections.

As a first approximation and rule of thumb, live, viable inventories will likely be less than 50% of what shows on the business's balance sheet. Sad, but true.

All balance sheet items, assets and liabilities need to be challenged. One thing easy to miss is the legal status of intellectual property used by the business. You need to know if there is legal access to needed intellectual property: patents, copyrights and trademarks. You also need to know the status of any intellectual property owned by the company. A good consultant is worth every penny you pay in this process of evaluation.

So, if you decide to acquire a business rather than start one from scratch, this has been a brief summary of the bare essentials of the process.

Whether you acquire an existing business or start one *de novo,* there are a few essentials that cannot be ignored. To be successful in a business career, one needs sharp tools, very sharp tools. The first and most indispensable is a good basic education in business fundamentals. That doesn't necessarily mean a college degree or an MBA but it does mean a good grasp of the organizational and financial information usually gained in a good college undergraduate business curriculum or an MBA program.

You cannot manage any business well, especially not a growing start-up business, without a basic understanding of accounting, tax, finance, management, business law and marketing. All of these skills can be provided by people you hire but if you personally lack a fundamental level of understanding and knowledge of the basics, someone else will eventually own your business, especially if you are successful.

I have known several entrepreneurs who have lost control of their creation as it moved strongly into the win column because they trusted others, both family members and outsiders who had become involved in the company. The founders were unable to personally grasp the details of the business and the business/political fundamentals necessary to maintain control of their creation. I will discuss the issue of control several times in the later chapters of this book as we discuss a variety of subjects from the *rules*.

Control is the holy grail of any business and especially an entrepreneurial business that you create.

Besides getting a good education, I personally recommend that you invest a few of your early working years, three to five years, with a relatively large, well-organized company to get some real-life experience in the basics of management. It might help to get into a company related to the field in which you think you want to be active later as an entrepreneur or in a closely related field. There are big benefits that flow from a solid grounding in established business practices before you venture out on your own. While it isn't absolutely necessary to have prior business experience, it significantly improves your odds of success.

Before I started my own business, I had spent four years in the Navy, two years at Texas Instruments and 17 years at Varo, Inc., in Texas. During my early years at Varo, I was responsible for a business start-up within a pre-existing business. Those early days at Varo were an incredibly good learning experience for me. I also spent considerable time working toward an MBA in night school which I did not complete. But in the incomplete educational process, I got a thorough grounding in the details of accounting, business law and marketing. I discovered that my on-the-job training, though I learned much from it, had left out many essential concepts that are treated in a business school program, which covers entire topics from cover to cover. Many business management schools (including the University of Texas at Dallas) now have specialized entrepreneurial programs designed specifically to prepare you for the business start-up battle!

The workplace alone will likely not give you the comprehensive treatment of all the relevant issues that may arise as your career progresses. To me it seems that you get a load of bricks in the workplace but you get the mortar gluing it all together in school.

On the other hand, in an existing business what you get is a real-world experience, quite different from the classroom. That is especially true when it comes to learning corporate politics. There will never be an organization without politics, so you might as well master the art. It will definitely help you if you become a skillful politician; I guarantee it.

JAN'S 50 *RULES* FOR THE ENTREPRENEUR

I urge you to use the following 50 rules as a checklist before you attempt to start a new business. You'll avoid many of the destructive issues that I have either seen or experienced throughout my 50-year business career observing and participating in entrepreneurial business start-ups. The chapters that follow will explain many of these *rules* and give examples of how a failure to be aware of the numerous pitfalls may result in unnecessarily difficult start-up problems in businesses, sometimes resulting in loss of ownership, loss of control and even bankruptcy.

The 12 most important rules:

1. *Success in a business venture requires several powerful personal qualities.* Without all of these you're unlikely to find total success. The almost indispensable qualities are: **Concept, Courage, Commitment, Capital and a tolerance for Risk.**

2. *Never become involved in a 50/50 partnership;* such arrangements are almost always unstable! You should be the boss/owner or the employee. As boss if there is an offending party in the business or a disagreement, you can fire the individual. If you are the employee, and you have a major disagreement, you can quit. Partners are stuck with each other and even with a buy/sell agreement at the outset, there is usually not a very attractive way to resolve

a partnership dispute. Likewise, any stock ownership less than 51% carries a big risk to you unless it is the stock in a large, publicly traded company. The exception to this rule is that it may be necessary to accept a minority or 50/50 position in order to make your first bit of wealth that will allow you to accumulate enough capital to start your own company.

3. You must be cautious to ensure that you have *adequate capital* to start with. Raising capital later will cost you dearly. The best source of capital is your own money and retained profits. Failure to have adequate capital at the outset will likely mean you will lose control of your company.

4. *You must choose your own mentors!* Having one or more good mentors is very helpful in starting a business. For that matter, mentors are essential in other areas such as a regular job or personal issues. If you think someone can help you, approach them and ask advice. Most people are willing to give their advice and in fact they feel flattered that you ask. If their advice is sound, you can go back to them later. You must acquire mentors the hard way: Ask them! Above all, *seek trustworthy advisers* who can challenge your personal myths.

5. *Set personal goals* for long, medium and short range. Always maintain an informal back-pocket escape plan (parachute) for unexpected disasters. Your escape plan is not a part of your business plan or your budget plan. It is just an escape plan! *An escape plan is necessary since even a good business plan can fail.* Good ideas are a dime a dozen . . . good ideas that will create a successful business are relatively rare. Beware of a plan that doesn't look very, very good when it is explained on one sheet of tablet paper. If a very careful sharp-pencil analysis is needed to show profitability, you may be in trouble.

6. Maintenance of ***voting control*** of your company is essential. Boards of directors may turn on you. If you do not have voting control, you're essentially an employee subject to the whims of the true owners.

7. ***Mismanagement of cash and inventory*** break more small companies than all other causes taken together. Companies that you consider for acquisition may have a large percentage of dead inventories. Careful due diligence before acquisition is critical! Starting a business is very hard work. Rare is the entrepreneur who does not work 10 to 12 hours a day and 6 to 7 days a week. ***If you don't like hard work, get a job***. In the words of President Harry Truman, "If you can't stand the heat stay out of the kitchen," or, be an airline pilot!

8. The ***80/20 rule*** applies in a start-up business, so beware of misuse of your time and all other assets. There are always distractions and they must be ignored.

9. There many aspects to starting a business, but ***cash flow management*** is critical. If you don't have a clear picture of how to do it, get good advice!

10. Allow your thinking about a new business to go ***beyond what you consider your limits.*** We all live in a box the walls of which are our own construction. Try to avoid the box, but if you can't, make the box really big.

11. ***Always demand an arbitration clause*** in any contract! (The American Arbitration Association can provide you with language for this clause.) Arbitration clauses provide a sensible, quick and relatively inexpensive method of dispute resolution. The arbitration panel member or members will usually be individuals who are smart and experienced in handling disputes and somewhat knowledgeable in your

business sector. Your lawyer may resist an arbitration clause, but don't be misled! Mediation and lawsuit are no substitute for arbitration unless you were unfortunate enough to not have an arbitration clause to begin with.

12. Do not depend on help from the **Uniform Commercial Code**. It might be helpful, but it may not. Arbitration clauses are the way to go to minimize the cost of settling disputes. A good lawyer is an indispensable asset to your efforts in entrepreneurship.

12 good habits necessary for starting a business:

1. **Procrastination** is not necessarily a problem. Usually procrastination is the result of your intuition telling you that something is wrong. Pay attention to your inner self!

2. **Intuition** is essentially the computer in your brain analyzing unlimited number of variables that don't necessarily come up to your conscious mind. Rational analysis always limits the number of variables. So, do not automatically disregard your intuition. Always leave room for **unexpected opportunity** in your budgeting and planning exercises.

3. Be careful to avoid **paralysis by analysis**. At some point you need to commit to a plan to move forward. Later revisions are appropriate; you'll never get it exactly right on the first try.

4. If you're planning to be an entrepreneur, **start saving 10% right now**. And, that's 10% right off the top. Otherwise you'll always be working for someone else's account. You will need at least two years personal expense reserve in the bank when you plan a start-up in addition to the capital needed for the business. According to a popular magazine,

the average age of a starting entrepreneur is about 40. The reason for that is that it takes a while for anyone to accumulate sufficient capital to start a business unless they have been lucky enough to inherit the money. On the other hand, many of the very young dot-com CEOs convinced investors to let them have vast sums of money and yet maintain control. That fad is probably gone forever.

5. Once your business is running, have your accountant or financial officer provide a *weekly financial report.* They probably won't like that idea but you must insist. Tell them that you understand that it will not be exactly accurate, but you need to know approximately where you're at all the time. Most critical are the disposition of assets, cash, inventory and accounts receivable. Bank loan availability figures on your revolving account are very important to you if you are running on some borrowed funds, and you almost certainly will be.

6. Remember, *it's not really profit until the check clears the bank.* Before that it's just an investment that may or may not pay off. Collecting accounts receivable is a tough job and many customers don't pay until they are asked several times. If you fail to call them, they may wait 90 or 120 days, or longer, to pay you.

7. In achieving the goals you set, you will find that by *measuring a person's performance,* the performance will improve. Any significant business measure that gets charted and visibly posted and that you look at frequently, will automatically improve. Posting a chart over a subordinate's desk, asking him to keep it up-to-date and then your checking it weekly will have profound effects. You should probably limit this approach to just one or two items for any given employee. But you must follow up and comment even if it's brief!

8. Pay careful attention to details *but don't lose sight of the big picture.*

9. *Don't panic*, it won't help!

10. Bill Moore, a well regarded Dallas area business consultant, has had as his motto for years, *"Focus and Execute."* I have adopted that motto and so should you. There is simply no substitute for personal discipline.

11. *Do not chase rabbits!* Any effort that is not leading to accomplishment of your goals is a waste of time, energy and resources. They shoot bird dogs that chase rabbits!

12. Once your company is up and running and profitable, *be careful of any "bet the company" ideas.*

7 Cautionary rules:

1. *Don't confuse entrepreneurship with recklessness.* Aggressiveness plus discipline is needed to make a successful entrepreneur or a great fighter pilot! An undisciplined entrepreneur goes broke. An undisciplined and reckless fighter pilot dies! Neither can succeed without a balanced combination of aggressiveness and discipline.

2. In any business, customers must be clearly identified through market research. *Without customers there is no business.*

3. *The pricing of your product or service is a critical aspect of your business.* Do not allow anyone but you to set prices! Note that a 1% reduction in price can lead to a 5% to 10% reduction and profitability on that contract. The pricing buck must stop with you! And don't be fooled by overly

eager salesmen, there'll be many times that you'll need to face down your customer when he has a gun pointed at your head. As Kenny Rogers said, "You gotta know when to hold 'em and know when to fold 'em"! And, as a great fighter pilot once said, "No guts, no glory!"

4. *The law of unintended consequences* is fundamental in any business. It is impossible to make a decision that changes just one thing. Frequently the other things that get changed are not obvious at the time of the decision. Customers and suppliers tend to be the source of many of these kinds of unexpected problems, and the customer is always right, well, almost always right!

5. *Enlarge your circle of contacts!* Good ideas can come from many directions. The more people you know, the greater the potential idea flow in your direction. People who think they have good luck have more acquaintances than losers. Large bases of acquaintances give you a huge pool in which to seek new mentors, you almost can't have too many. And, I don't mean looking for mentors on a golf course. Golf is the enemy of the new business since it sucks up so much time. Join the Rotary Club or a church or some hobby group.

6. I urge you to *read and believe* Lateral Thinking for Management, a book written by Edward de Bono while he was in charge of education at General Electric many years ago. Newer editions of the book are available on Amazon. com. I think I got more value out of this one book than any other management book I've ever read. It is especially helpful for the new entrepreneur.

7. How many times have you heard the phrase "you need to make a decision and stick with it!" This advice is simply nuts. *One of the best things you can do is quickly reverse a*

bad decision. Trying to live with a bad decision is almost instant business suicide. Situations change frequently and you have to change with them! On the other hand, being wishy-washy and capricious will result in utter confusion for your customers and your subordinates. So, a balance must be struck.

19 Leadership rules:

1. ***Most of these remaining rules will focus on personal behavior***, yours, your associates, your customers, your investors, if any, and your bank. ***Absolute honesty*** is required when you report any information to any of these people, it must be the whole truth and nothing but the truth. There will be times when you may be tempted to spin the numbers . . . don't do it! It will kill you in the long run!

2. ***Be on time.*** Even if you are the owner of the company, be on time. Tardiness demonstrates a lack of personal discipline or possibly arrogance, or both. Be on time!

3. ***Maintain a sense of humor.*** Even though business should be quite serious, there is always room for humor and it can lighten up any tense situation.

4. ***Be willing to listen to all your associates***, but the final decisions must be yours.

5. ***Fairness*** in all your dealings will serve you well in business and at home.

6. ***Any employee you decide you must terminate*** should probably have been terminated 6 to 12 months earlier. You will find that a good firing raises morale. You will be the last person in the company to know that someone is

not meeting the standards. Everyone else will already have seen it and wondered why it took you so long.

7. ***Work should be fun for everyone***. If it's not, the individual is in the wrong job. Try to make work fun for all of your associates.

8. ***Be inclusive!*** An individual not invited to provide advice in forming a decision may not be very anxious to execute the decision. Meetings can waste a lot of time, but unfortunately they are essential. Every meeting should end with a do list, most importantly, a next step for everybody involved.

9. ***Your employees must be trained and you must delegate*** the work to them and follow up! You need to become a great "have-doner," not a great "doer"! If it is to be a successful business, you can't do it all by yourself. See William Oncken's classic, *Management time, who's got the monkey,* available from Amazon.com. This book will absolutely clarify the task of delegation in your mind and in the minds of any of your supervisory personnel.

10. ***Never ask anyone to do something that you wouldn't do!*** This is a key aspect of good leadership.

11. You must convince your salesmen to ***spend almost as much time selling their ideas inside the company*** as with customers on the outside. Everyone, from the executive suite to the stockroom, must buy-in on a complex sale or it will backfire.

12. Be careful of the orders you give. If they are too narrowly drawn, the result may be ***"malicious obedience."*** The order may be executed exactly as given even when it is clearly seen by the employee to be defective. "I only did

what you told me to do, boss." I would fire any employee immediately who pulled this trick. On the other hand, be careful how you give orders.

13. I would suggest to any executive that **he/she place his/ her own phone calls,** especially to customers or the bank. There is no more profound way to express arrogance and contempt than having a secretary place a phone call and ask the individual on the other line to "Please hold for Mr. Big"! I have always been tempted to hang up on this kind of call! Maybe it's just me . . .

14. **Never invent when you can copy.** There are great ideas out there everywhere. Of course, you must not infringe on others' intellectual property.

15. **Morale is follower.** The CEO must be the leader! When results improve, morale improves automatically. Good leadership can generate good teamwork which can generate good results and then good morale.

16. I have found that **handwritten notes** delivered by US mail are far more effective than phone calls or e-mails when you are attempting to thank someone or send condolences. Email is very fast but it is very impersonal. There are dozens of other methods of communication these days, but US mail is still a good one, less than $.50 for a live stamp. That's a cheap price for a dose of good will.

17. **Don't take yourself too seriously**, a bit of self-deprecating humor can come in handy.

18. **Be sure to leave some time for play.** Fresh air and exercise are good for your mental health. Spend time with your family, they deserve it. A vacation now and then is essential.

19. And finally, ***the most important rule:*** The quest for wealth alone may not be enough for you to get started, but entrepreneurial success will lead to wealth more reliably than almost any other path . . . so,

Go start something!

GREAT ENTREPRENEURS

A beginning entrepreneur can learn a lot by observing other successful entrepreneurs. Take every chance to visit entrepreneurial enterprises and try to get to know some of the successful people who have started and operated them. Their habits are worth emulating. Just a bit of Internet research will provide you with a huge amount of data on successful companies.

Southwest Airlines has been one of the most successful entrepreneurial ventures of modern times. Southwest was started by two bright young men, a pilot and a lawyer. Southwest was started with a minimum of capital, three airplanes and barely enough money to operate, but the founders had a really big vision. Early in their corporate life, they even had to sell one of their planes to raise cash during crunch time. While they may have been short on capital, they were long on concept, commitment and courage, plus an abundance of chutzpah! Southwest's founders and management also had the most necessary ingredient for the entrepreneur, a positive mental attitude! I mention more about mental attitude later.

Herb Kelleher, a lawyer and one of the two key founders, even hawked company stock shares at a booth at the State Fair of Texas to raise operating funds. Nevertheless, in spite of many difficulties, Southwest grew and Herb and the management team he assembled built one of the most successful enterprises in America. Southwest was almost undone in the early stages due to a shortage of capital but they managed to overcome. Adequate capital is very critical to all companies but especially to start-ups.

Southwest crept into the airline business amid vicious political resistance and years of litigation. There were massive efforts attempting to block Southwest's access to its home base, Dallas Love Field. Southwest's management survived the lawsuits and continued a process of slowly leveraging their very limited capital and borrowing capacity as they developed the business. Southwest is now one of the top airlines in the United States, or in the world for that matter.

Southwest came into existence in the late '60s and successfully developed the intra-state market for air transportation in Texas. By serving only Texas, Southwest avoided the federal regulatory system that was operated by the Civil Aeronautics Board. At that time, the CAB allotted routes and set ticket pricing within the National Air Transportation System.

Love Field proved to be unique in that it was supplanted by a much larger airport in 1974, the Dallas/Fort Worth International Airport midway between Dallas and Fort Worth. All of the airlines in existence in 1968 had signed contracts to relocate their services to the new airport when it opened. Since Southwest did not exist at the time of the contract signing, they were not a signatory and refused to leave Love Field in 1974. Southwest's refusal to relocate to the new airport became the focus of an intense political and legal battle with the other airlines, the two cities of Dallas and Fort Worth which had financed the new airport, DFW airport. Through years of court action there was a determined effort to force SWA to relocate to DFW and/or block their use of Love Field.

When airline deregulation was passed by Congress in 1978, there was huge concern that Southwest might now provide service for all of the United States from Love Field. If so, the major airlines might need to retreat from DFW International to Love Field to remain competitive. Sensing a major disaster for the western half of the metropolitan area, specifically Fort Worth, Congressman Jim Wright wrote an amendment, known as the Wright Amendment, which restricted Southwest's nonstop operations from Love Field to destinations in Texas and the four states bordering Texas. A new ticket and rechecking of luggage was required to fly into the rest of the United States from any of those adjacent-state destinations.

In the period from 2006 to 2008, intense negotiations brought about the successful end to the Wright Amendment. While the final chapter ending the Wright Amendment will not be complete until eight years after the multi-party agreement, significant improvements in the status of commercial aviation in the Dallas-Fort Worth area were achieved. I had the pleasure of being Chairman of the Board for DFW International Airport during this period.

One of the most important keys to Southwest's continuing success has been their strict attention to a clear mission plan and an incredibly positive mental attitude. The "Southwest Spirit" is required for every member of the Southwest team from the top to the bottom. If new recruits are deemed incapable of maintaining this positive mental attitude, they're usually not hired by Southwest. Southwest's operating focus has from the beginning been short-haul routes using just one aircraft type, the legendary Boeing 737. Southwest has never wavered from this operating philosophy. All pilots, flight crews, gate crews, baggage crews and maintenance technicians are capable of working on any of their aircraft. In contrast, some airlines have seven or eight different types of aircraft and support equipment which vastly complicates the management, maintenance and scheduling challenges for the airline.

Aircraft diversity is usually required for a combination of domestic and international service. Examples of diversified airlines are American Airlines and Delta. Southwest functions only in the

USA. This may change in the near future as Southwest continues to develop new routes, perhaps to Mexico and beyond. So far, Southwest's focus on domestic short-haul passenger traffic with one type aircraft has been their key to more than 40 years of amazing, highly profitable growth and marketing success while many other airlines, both start-ups and mature legacy carriers, went bankrupt.

In my opinion, the incredible success of Southwest Airlines, from their very beginning, is closely related to their intensely positive mental attitude. There are few attributes more vital to an entrepreneur. Herb Kelleher is the best example of great positive mental attitude that I have ever known. Southwest also does a remarkable job of employee recognition, a key to great morale. I think Southwest Airlines presents an excellent model to any entrepreneurial business, large or small.

Another good friend of mine, Bob Alpert, a towering example of positive mental attitude and a successful real estate entrepreneur, shared an interesting quote with me a few years ago: "A dollar borrowed is a dollar earned, and a dollar paid back is a dollar lost forever!" I am not sure Bob coined that quote, but it is a good one! The use of leveraged debt can be an essential element in any new and growing business and is absolutely essential in the real estate business. However, leverage can viciously cut both ways: You can win big but you can lose even bigger, as happened to many busted real estate entrepreneurs in Texas in the early eighties. But, it is clear to me that the clever use of leverage and a positive mental attitude are the ham and eggs for the entrepreneur.

The Dallas region, my home, is filled with incredible examples of highly successful entrepreneurs throughout the twentieth century.

Many of the businesses that we enjoy today in our everyday life started as entrepreneurial ventures with no assurance of success. Norman Brinker started a restaurant in Dallas: Steak and Ale. He used that first restaurant in Dallas to develop a formula that he later spread far and wide. Brinker eventually sold Steak and Ale to Pillsbury but he then used those funds to build an even more massive food service enterprise, Brinker International, with Chili's Restaurants headlining the company. He later introduced many other great food names that we see almost everywhere in America today.

A number of years ago, my wife and I visited a new start-up restaurant concept of Brinker's, Macaroni Grill, just after it had opened. We were stunned to see Norm Brinker (by then a big-time CEO) sitting at a customer table located near the kitchen where he could observe every server's activity. He had a notepad and a number of other documents at hand. We walked back to say hello and find out what he was doing. The answer: Norm was looking for improvements in the service quality and the efficiency in his new restaurant concept. He did not send a staff person to do that job; he was doing it himself because he took personal responsibility for service excellence in his hundreds of restaurants. He demanded the job be done right on his newly acquired restaurant chain! Needless to say, as a direct result of Norm's careful attention to detail, the Macaroni Grill restaurant chain and all of the other Brinker restaurants have been highly successful.

One of the defining characteristics of a successful entrepreneur is his or her total commitment to detail and perfection in quality and service to customers. Anything less will lead to mediocrity, or worse, total failure. There <u>*is*</u> *no business without happy customers!*

Stanley Marcus, of Neiman-Marcus, showed us all how to do top-end consumer retailing. He insisted on complete customer satisfaction. He was extreme in this pursuit and his customers willingly paid more to get first-class products and service. Wealthy people from the world over traveled to Dallas just to shop in his stores. Stanley wrote several books and many articles based on his merchandising wisdom. He insisted on complete customer satisfaction. All of his employees were imbued with this same ethic.

Stanley Marcus would stand high on any list of great entrepreneurs. If you are in the retail business his books are **must reads!**

Mary Kay Ash, another Dallas entrepreneur, formed one of the most dynamic cosmetic companies in the world, Mary Kay Cosmetics. She pioneered the mass personal-marketing concept for cosmetics. Her thousands of sales associates worshiped the very ground she walked on. Her use of pink Cadillacs as a sales incentive is legendary. Proud was the saleswoman driving one of these pink icons! These ladies would work tirelessly to get one of those cars at the big annual Mary Kay convention. That same hard work propelled Mary Kay Cosmetics into the stratosphere. Only a few people that I ever met had a greater positive mental attitude than Mary Kay Ash.

Ross Perot, Sr., built not one, but two incredibly successful computer service companies in Dallas. His son, Ross Perot, Jr., has gone on to create a huge real estate enterprise with new ventures all around the world. Ross Sr. climbed onto his surfboard just as the computer services monster wave in the 1960s, one of the biggest waves ever, crested under him. He quickly became one of the richest men in the world at the time. He had the right idea at the right time and the faith, ultra-positive mental attitude and boundless fortitude to make it happen.

Roger Staubach, the finest quarterback in the history of the Naval Academy and the leader of the legendary Dallas Cowboys "America's Team," has gone on since Super Bowl fame to create a massive international real estate enterprise in his post-football phase of life. Roger pioneered the concept of actually representing the interests of the tenant in real estate dealings. Up to that time, most deals were done in the interest of the property owner since he was the one who was paying the commission! Roger changed the game and has had huge successes as a direct result. I do not need to say much about Roger's positive mental attitude; his stunning fourth-quarter comebacks offer adequate proof. He has been a first-class entrepreneur. The same personal qualities and determination that made Roger such an incredible athlete propelled him forward in his entrepreneurial efforts. No one turns down a phone call from Roger! How would you like to have a door-opener like that?

Other Dallas real estate entrepreneurial icons include Raymond Nasher, Trammell Crow, Henry Beck and Henry Miller, all with major properties across America and around the world. Ebby Halliday, one of the early female entrepreneurs in our region, stands out as another Dallas legend. She built one of the nation's top residential real estate brokerages, a major achievement for a female starting a business in Dallas in the forties. She began her meteoric real estate career more than sixty years ago, testimony to the long life of a good idea perfectly executed. She stressed the personal touch with her customers and recognized that it was the wife who made the home-buying decisions! Her company was one of the first female-owned and -operated entrepreneurial companies in America at that time. But, she saw a strong customer need and filled it. At age 99, she still comes to the office every day and is involved in many civic affairs. I visited with her several months ago and she told me she still had her driver's license . . . I asked her if she still drove. She said yes . . . but, no one would ride with her! What a lady! She is an inspiration to all of us.

During the early years of the huge East Texas oil boom, H.L. Hunt started with little more than grit and guts and built a massive fortune in the oil industry. It wasn't always an upward trip for him. He weathered boom and bust but kept on going in spite of the hardships in the oil patch, where a run of dry holes can put you out of business really quickly. Today, one of his sons, Ray Hunt, controls the huge Hunt Consolidated Company headquartered in Dallas. Along with the oil business, he has developed many other real estate and hotel businesses plus a burgeoning venture capital group. Hunt Oil, his flagship operating company, does exploration and development throughout the Americas and the rest of the world finding and producing black gold. It may have been a humble start for H.L. Hunt, but he was near the very beginning of a new industry and he survived and eventually thrived, as have his several sons.

Another great Dallas area entrepreneurial story not widely publicized is the amazing success of Dan Flaherty and his wife, Dannie. While graduate students at the University of Dallas in the eighties, they conceived the idea of novelty products based on the then brand-new talking-chip technology being developed in the semiconductor industry. While their company, Gemmie Industries, has now marketed many products, undoubtedly their most well-known hit product was "Billy Bass," the singing and swimming largemouth black bass! There were a number of other fish species that they made sing too. They saw the opportunity to take advantage of new technology in computer-generated voice chips. They have continued to innovate in technology-driven novelties, with a large engineering force in the Dallas area and more than 20,000 manufacturing employees in China.

These brilliant Texas entrepreneurs, and all American entrepreneurs, deserve your study. Most of them started small with a good idea, a dream and an incredible "can-do" positive mental attitude. I cannot imagine a successful entrepreneur who did not have an extremely positive attitude. It is an essential ingredient. Seek entrepreneurs whom you can use as a guide. They are around you and you only need to look.

Corollary: In my opinion, pessimists rarely, if ever, accomplish anything.

So, when you get up in the mornings, put on your white hat, set your course for the day and move out with great enthusiasm, confidence and a positive mental attitude. You cannot win if you do not play! And, you have to play hard!

So, go start something!

CHAPTER 2

MY EARLY YEARS

I started my adult life in the mid-1950s after two years in a local community college, Arlington State College. I received an associate degree in industrial mechanical engineering. I wanted to be a Navy pilot and at that time, 60 hours of college was required to enter the Naval Flight Cadet program. My two years generated those 60+ hours. Immediately after graduation, I joined the U.S. Navy and went to Pensacola, Florida. Eighteen months later I graduated from flight training, winning my coveted Wings of Gold.

At that point, I married my high-school sweetheart, Suzanne McKevitt. She made the mistake of marrying a "hot" pilot flying Navy jet fighters who had just turned 21. We have stayed together for over 55 years!

Before I joined, I did not have a great deal of knowledge about the Navy, but found it to be one of the oldest, largest and best-organized entities (and bureaucracies) in the world. As a civilian pilot, I still deeply enjoy the privilege of my participation in many Naval Air Station airshows around the country. I entertain the crowds as a "stunt pilot," flying a high-tech single-engine hotrod, the Extra-300L, an aerobatic plane built in Germany.

If you have seen the movie *An Officer and a Gentleman* (and if not, call Netflix), you know what I went through in pre-flight school.

I had grown up in a lower-middle-class neighborhood and when I graduated from Jesuit High School, I had a relatively low level of personal expectation. None of my family, even my extended family, had attended college. Only a very few had had any military experience, mostly draftees in World War II.

You can learn a lot of things in any military service branch. The Navy was my choice. I liked the idea of landing on an aircraft carrier. During World War II, I had read a book on dive bombers that really caught my imagination! Dive bombing was one of the key methods of aerial combat and anti-ship attacks used by the Navy during the "big war." I decided then that was what I wanted to do. As it turned out, I ended up flying fighters rather than bombers.

I do not know of anyone who can't personally profit from military experience. From day-one, the Navy toughened me up, broadened my worldview and gave new purpose to my life in a way that no other experience could have. A military flight program, regardless of whether it is Army, Navy or Air Force, demands an extremely positive mental attitude just to get into it.

The Navy turned out to be a major maturing experience for me. I needed the guidance and structure that the Navy Flight Program offered. But the most important thing I learned during my four years of active service in the Navy, besides self-discipline, was that I needed a college degree! Few people succeeded as naval officers without a college degree. So I opted out of active duty after four years, but continued eight more years flying in the reserves while I worked and attended night school at the University of Texas at Arlington.

Once out of the Navy, my first civilian job was at Texas Instruments (1958), a then moderate-sized entrepreneurial high-tech company in the newly emerging semiconductor field. I didn't purposely seek this job and knew nothing about the company. But by that time, at age 23, I had a wife and two very young daughters and I needed employment! Not long after that we had a third daughter.

My job at TI was at the very bottom of the food chain. It was a humbling experience to move from the glamorous job of a Navy Jet Fighter Pilot to such a low-level civilian job, job grade 01, the absolute bottom of the TI pecking order. But, humility is a good trait for the entrepreneur and I certainly got a good dose of that at Texas Instruments.

One major lesson: You can learn something from everyone and in every situation if you pay attention.

I used every available minute at TI to absorb the nature of the business and the technology. I was an engineering wanna-be already and this was engineering heaven. I pursued a technical degree for several years in night school, financed partially by the GI Bill. I finally got a B.S. degree in Math and Physics from the University of Texas at Arlington in 1963, after five years of intense effort while holding full-time jobs, flying in the reserves and helping my wife raise our three young daughters, all of whom attended my college graduation. I look back at that experience now and wonder how it was possible. I guess I was young and eager. And there was really no other alternative if I wanted to get an education and support my family at the same time. Thankfully, I have always had a strong PMA (positive mental attitude).

While I was flying in the Navy Reserve, I was lucky to have a few years flying the amazing Chance Vought F8U Crusader, the first truly supersonic jet fighter designed for naval carrier aviation. That was a real blast, 1000 mph plus!

In the meantime, and a couple of years before I graduated from college, I had moved on from Texas Instruments to a smaller company, Varo Inc., in Garland, Texas, near Dallas. There, I started an internal semiconductor manufacturing operation to support a military contract that the company had just won. The product my new semiconductor division supported was the incredible, see-in-the-dark, Starlight Scope, made famous in Vietnam. This was my first almost-entrepreneurial opportunity but I didn't know exactly how to grasp it. I couldn't even spell *entrepreneur*! I just took the job and did my best. I became a reasonably well-paid engineer and manager, and built a very successful company-within-a-company which eventually overshadowed the parent in the early 1970s. I became the Chairman and CEO of the rapidly growing and very profitable subsidiary, Varo Semiconductor, Inc., in 1971, as a result of serious profitability problems in the parent company.

The result was that my semiconductor operation made a huge profit . . . but it was for **someone else's account!**

I ended up being ejected from the company in 1978 due mostly to my sense of independence and refusal to play the role of a subordinate to the Chairman and CEO of the parent company with whom I had nothing in common. I was actually the president of the parent corporation at the time, a NYSE firm, but not the CEO. The key element I was missing was **CONTROL**.

After my departure from Varo, a company in which I had invested seventeen precious years of my life, I decided to fend off the numerous headhunters for six months in order to have time to decide what I really wanted to do with the rest of my life. At age 44, I decided that I didn't want to immediately go back into a situation where a board of directors or a chairman could take control of my life. I drove around Texas alone for a couple of weeks visiting a few cattle feeding lots and doing some photography to clear my head so that I could begin to do a little "thinking outside of the box."

A quiet time for personal introspection is an important element for those who have been driven nearly crazy by an intense corporate experience. It takes time to get past the numbness that even small bureaucracies develop in you.

Eventually, I realized that there had to be a better way forward than taking another job, even as a CEO.

A good friend and fellow member of the Young Presidents Organization approached me with some vital counseling that was invaluable to my awakening to the real entrepreneurial opportunities that abounded. He took me around to several of the small companies he owned showing me the value that could be had by owning small private companies.

I spent some quality time with him for a few days and he showed me some of the secrets he had learned the hard way. I want to share some of those "secrets" with you in this book along with many more that I have learned over the last 30-plus years as an independent entrepreneur.

He emphasized the idea *that wealth flows only from a personally owned business, never from a job.*

That one idea is the most important idea in this book!

Your life may be very satisfying as an employee, and if you think that's a good plan for life, *stop reading right here!* But if you seek real wealth and, far more importantly, true satisfaction in your work, read on.

I may not have *the* secret formula, but the ideas expressed here will give you a giant head start on the road to an entrepreneurial lifestyle and the personal wealth that can be created. More importantly, these ideas may set you on a path to the highest level of personal achievement: self actualization (see Maslow's pyramid, *the hierarchy of values*).

My YPO "guru" showed me an article in the local newspaper about a Dallas area public company CEO who had earned $400,000 in the past year. This was 1978, when $400,000 was a lot of money for a public-company CEO! The newspaper article was self-righteously critical and suggested that the fellow was vastly overcompensated. My friend confided with me that he had earned almost $4,000,000 in the same year and nobody had any idea of who he was or how much he had earned. He could run below the radar and spend Friday afternoon in the local country club card room. He had no board of directors nor angry stockholders who might complain. The local business writers didn't even know his name. This relative anonymity may actually be one of the main benefits of an entrepreneurial business. He urged me to forget the "corporate world" and to *go start something*.

I want you to consider doing the same!

I spent the next six months pondering the future and deciding what the rest of my life would be like. I came up with four long-range goals. Here is what I determined was my vision and dream:

1. I would stay in Dallas Texas, my home and my best base of support.
2. I would stay in electronics, as I had twenty years experience in the semiconductor field.
3. I would want the business to be international since I like to travel.
4. And, most importantly, no matter how small it might be, **it would be all mine!**

"It would be all mine" dominated my decision-making and governed the size of my start-up, since I had a relatively limited amount of personal capital. But I was committed to having just one board member: Me! I put my entire net worth on the line. If I failed, it was back to job hunting and a lifetime status as an employee, not an owner. Now that's motivation!

Goal setting was not new to me but it took on a new importance, since every hour of effort and every dollar of capital was precious. I will address the important issue of goal setting in a later chapter. I taped my goals inside a desk drawer where I would be forced to see them almost daily. I vowed that my new business might be small but it would definitely be all mine; **I would make it or break it!**

I got great support from my wife and three daughters but I don't think they understood the magnitude of the risk. By that time my children were all in college and did not experience the day-to-day trauma of the start-up. That was lucky for them. I did my best to keep a positive attitude any time I talked about the business. There was no need for them to share my concerns.

I worked hard, determined to succeed, and set high targets in my monthly goals!

As you will see later in this book, you must get into the habit of setting personal goals, written goals, in order to have the best chance for success. If goals are not written, they don't count. I cannot overemphasize the importance of written goals: long-range and annual, monthly, or even weekly goals and checklists when time is critical.

I set, wrote and met most of my 1978 goals and my goals for every year thereafter. I had a 25-year run of successful business up to the point that I sold my companies and semi-retired. But even though I'm almost retired now, I still set written personal goals every year and I will continue to write my annual goals as long as I can.

I always carry a list of to-do items in my shirt pocket. For years, I used 3x5 index cards. After a few years I had special cards printed with rounded corners to stop the "dog-earing" of the 3x5s. I recommend this to you regardless of how good your memory is. PDAs, computers, iPhones and other electronic devices are great, but the checklist card in your shirt pocket is still a good idea. I have always kept a long-term file for my used to-do lists and my pocket cards. They make interesting reading and sometimes they can provide important references. I also retain all of my personal calendars and as many business records as possible. Everyone has a different approach to record retention, but you never know when you might need to recall specific times or events. Your follow-up lists and all of your records, if well-kept, will be of considerable help when you do the year-end review of your goals. Another approach, one that I have not used except occasionally, is a personal diary.

Our company, Collmer Semiconductor, achieved almost $60,000,000 in total annual sales in its last year. I might add that the company made more profit in its best quarters than I had made in cumulative salary and bonuses in my 20 years as an employee at TI and Varo . . . and I was the president of Varo Semiconductor for the final seven years and president of the whole corporation, Varo Inc., for the last two years!

Salaries just don't lead to personal wealth. A personally-owned business might.

After three very trying years of start-up investment, our company made a profit every year thereafter until I sold it. Before I started my own company, I had also made a profit for 68 consecutive quarters at Varo Semiconductor until I left in 1978; that profit was for the account of a lot of thankless managers and faceless stockholders. I got no really significant financial share of that effort. That's not a complaint, that's just an observation, and is the inevitable result of being an employee rather than an owner.

By the way, in a new business, I cannot over-emphasize the importance of careful selection of the first employees. I was extremely lucky to have the likes of Jim Mathis, Cathy Gorman, Sherry and Jerry Gallagher, Reggie Scheu, Gene Uecker, David Seals and many other great employees in my business. Those early years in the business were the greatest years of my life! We all had strong goals and strong positive mental attitudes. We set corporate goals and did a lot of contingency planning. We were an invincible team. Everybody did their best!

I've recounted my own personal experiences in starting a business and they are not unique. On the other hand, every entrepreneurial start-up is different. Careful study is essential to making your own personal decisions about your goals and objectives.

Be sure to set goals, long and short range. You may not accomplish them but they give you a target to shoot at. Without a target, you may be shooting aimlessly and accomplishing little.

Go start something!

If you do, the rewards, if any, will flow to YOUR account, and the accounts of your close associates, and not to a bunch of strangers.

STARTING SOMETHING

There are many things to consider in starting a business. In this chapter we will look at five of the most important personal issues that must be part of your plan: the four big Cs—Concept, Courage, Commitment, Capital—and the fifth and most critical item, a tolerance for Risk; risk is always present in a new business start-up.

I don't want to paint too rosy a picture for the beginning entrepreneur. Starting a company is not easy and it will stress you and your family to the max. Survival is never guaranteed. Many things must be done right to even get to first base. There are licenses, customers, products, sales, bookkeeping, taxes and a myriad of other difficult challenges to overcome and then, finally, you must make a profit! Profit is not automatic. But profit is the key to survival and growth of any start-up company. The corollary to profitability is the avoidance of losses. If you can avoid loss and keep a small momentum going, profit may eventually come. To generate the rewards of a personal business you must constantly keep your eye on profitability and maintain control to avoid losses if at all possible.

Avoiding loss is one of the keys to survival. But profit is the key to growth. Continuing profits put you on a solid path to wealth! Lack of profit is a fast track to "re-boot." Some failures are predictable. The entrepreneur who starts spending his money on personal perks before there is a solidly established business is almost certain to fail. In my opinion, there is little room for personal perks at any stage of a business. We were selling on a national basis and we traveled a lot. I never traveled any other way but coach and I expected my traveling salesmen and engineers to do the same. If your employees travel coach, so should you. The best training tool is example. If you waste company money, even though it is yours to waste, don't expect your people to be careful in their spending habits. If your work ethic is weak, theirs will be the same when you are not looking. In my opinion, the most basic element of leadership is never asking other people to do what you yourself won't do.

I had a couple of friends who extracted a $20 million cash investment from a French venture capital group in the early '80s to begin production of a new class of high-tech semiconductor chips. I was invited to visit their new world-class facility near Dallas. When I pulled up in the parking lot I was almost blinded by the sun's glare off the seven brand-new Cadillacs parked in reserved spots at the front door. This was a clear sign of oncoming disaster!

They blew through the twenty million in a few months and then succeeded in getting the French investor to send $18 million more. The whole operation lasted for about 18 months before liquidation. All of their high-tech equipment ended up in China.

The Cadillac/Mercedes/BMW syndrome is an advance warning for massive failure. It's so easy to predict. Employees will be as loose as the leadership is in their expenditures. Every penny in a start-up is critical. Any form of waste simply cannot be tolerated. And the entrepreneur has to lead the way. You may not be personally living in poverty, but you must absolutely avoid any excess in your business or personal expenditures. I remember visiting Tektronix Corporation headquarters in Oregon. They had no closed private offices. While I couldn't quite do that, the idea is a good one. You certainly do not want to present an air of personal arrogance in your company.

About the only areas where high style might be in order are some forms of consumer-related businesses, such as insurance or real estate, where consumer confidence in the salesman is very important. In these types of businesses, you must look the part of a successful businessperson; proper offices, stylish clothing and new cars may be essential elements for effective sales programs.

In any case, arriving at a final decision to actually start a business from scratch is a very difficult and even frightening step. There is no good way to do it gradually and succeed. A start-up requires your absolute commitment and your willingness to devote more than full-time work to the effort including all of your energy and focus. On the other hand, occasionally, people do succeed in starting up a small venture part-time while still drawing a paycheck elsewhere. I don't really recommend this approach, but one must make one's own decisions and live with life's limitations. Usually, a start-up involves seven days a week, 16 hours a day and intense mental effort on the part of the entrepreneur.

Adequate capital is essential to a start-up. Nevertheless, if you have the capacity for hard work, it is far better to start a business on a shoestring than to not start one at all!

While I promised to avoid suggesting businesses to look at, I do have a few observations on the process of business evaluations. Many ideas can be evaluated quickly for feasibility. The more opportunities considered, the better the final choice is likely to be. The role of luck will be discussed later. Luck is a major factor in our lives and it may make the difference in the choice of the business you decide to start. Luck might even make the difference between your success and failure.

While a quick analysis of a business idea can lead to a bad decision, a first look without commitment can shed a lot of light on a business idea. If it looks bad early on, look out, it may just be a bad idea. If it takes a sharp-pencil analysis to make you think you can scrape by, you may be in trouble before you start.

A prominent attorney and another of my personal gurus, Jim Donohoe, told me once that you should be able to summarize any business proposal on one sheet of yellow tablet paper with a blunt pencil. If the deal doesn't look like an incredibly profitable opportunity based on that one page, it probably won't work at all. No amount of analysis will make a bad deal work. Gut instincts or intuitions are great allies in this decision process. In any new business consideration, there needs to be some soaking time before you commit. From a thinking point of view, you need to try to visualize yourself actually *in* the business. Put on the new "hat" and see how it fits after a while. A bad idea will stink after a few days. Any idea will tend to look better at first glance than it does after some contemplation and study. So take your time! Don't rush into an error that may break you financially.

Herb Kelleher, the legendary CEO and founder of Southwest Airlines, tells the story of how he put the whole concept for the airline on a napkin at dinner with his co-founder, experienced airline pilot Rollin King. That napkin is still enshrined on the wall of the Dallas headquarters of Southwest Airlines. That may have been the shortest business plan of all time. Today Southwest Airlines is one of the pre-eminent airlines in America. All from that napkin! A six-foot bronze replica of that original "napkin plan" hangs in the SWA section of the Frontiers of Flight Museum at Dallas Love Field.

But while an initial business concept may be relatively simple and look good at first, bringing a business to life is a deeply complicated process. Kelleher, King and their backers sweated hard in the early days. No business starts by itself. Earlier I mentioned the story about Herb being at the State Fair of Texas selling Southwest Airlines stock from a booth. Now that's entrepreneurship! It also is a great example of Herb's determination, PMA, and his incredibly creative mind and "people sense." No self-effacing prank is beyond his ability or willingness to pull off.

Southwest has to be one of the best companies in the world in dealing with their employees, suppliers and especially, their customers. Herb is not afraid to throw a few bags in the luggage rack from time to time or hand out bags of peanuts on any SWA flight he happens to be on. The antics of all the cabin crews on Southwest Airlines are legendary. They insist that all employees have the "Spirit of Southwest Airlines." Southwest Airlines is a good model to study for any management team. I can't overstress the need for a positive mental attitude if you try to start a business.

Business ventures, especially entrepreneurial ventures, are as variable as the weather. Still, there are a number of important considerations that should be reviewed at various points along the way to start-up. My list of **rules** can serve as a vital **checklist** for you, the emerging entrepreneur. Each of these **rules**, and perhaps others I haven't thought of, may need your consideration, whether you decide to proceed or not.

When you get down to the actual effort of detailing a new business plan, your dreams may begin to evaporate. Bringing a dream to life is never easy. But a dream is absolutely essential to your future success. If you don't dream, you have no chance at all. These **rules for the entrepreneur** will at least give you a template to test your dreams against the raw realities of a business start-up and help you to adjust both your dream and your reality until you have a clear path to follow. Still, confusion and "the fog of war" are endemic to any business start-up. With a review of these **rules,** you might be able to cut through some of the fog, but after you have done that, you must then trust your own abilities to get a new venture going. Focus and execute!

In addition to the *rules*, which are just a checklist, there are five other absolute requirements for the adventure-minded, budding entrepreneur: the four big "Cs" and the one critical "R":

1. **Concept**
2. **Courage**
3. **Commitment**
4. **Capital**
5. **Risk**

No new venture is likely to succeed unless solutions to these five conditions are solidly in place. Some of the *rules* address the Cs indirectly. The R will be with you throughout the life of your enterprise. While many of the *rules* may not be relevant to a specific venture, there is no avoiding the four Cs and the big R since they are all essential ingredients to any successful venture. The four Cs are implicit throughout the *rules*. The R is omnipresent.

The four "Cs" are the *sine qua non* of venturing. In fact, the very word "venture" sums it all up; *to venture* means to have a concept, to display courage, to make a commitment, and to have capital! There is an old saying: ***Nothing ventured, nothing gained.***

Venturing is as old as humanity and it is a noble cause. Christopher Columbus was a great entrepreneur. His **concept** was that the earth was round and that a shorter and less expensive route to India and the spice trade was out there just waiting to be discovered. Columbus's concept was in direct conflict with the notion of a flat earth (though most serious scientists of the day recognized the roundness of the earth). But his was still a great concept: to prove the earth is round by discovering a shorter route to the spice-rich continent of India! Further, he had an abundance of **courage**, **commitment** and Queen Isabella's **capital,** all of which resulted in the surprise finding of a New World. There were certainly naysayers at that time who predicted that Columbus would sail off the edge of the earth. Columbus demonstrated extreme courage in the face of a lot of negative thinking. He certainly demonstrated absolute commitment, even into the extended portion of his voyage when his crew was turning against him. He took on more **risk** than most entrepreneurs could possibly encounter today.

You will have naysayers in your life who will solemnly predict that you will slip off the edge. You must tune them out! Admiral Farragut said it best, **"damn the torpedoes, full speed ahead!"** Our challenges today may be a bit more modest, but still, we must be intrepid adventurers to reap the rewards that are out there!

In addition to the four Cs, there can be no worthwhile venture without the **"R"** word: **Risk**. The very best you can hope to do is to minimize risk; it simply cannot be avoided in a venture. And that's where the courage comes into play. You must have the courage to risk failure in order to have a chance for a major score. Your capital, and perhaps your reputation, is what you have to lose if you fail. Columbus and many of the earlier explorers risked their lives. You probably will not have to go quite that far along the risk curve.

A venture, almost by definition, cannot have an early comfort zone. The risks are real and the process has its scary side, sometimes very scary. The prospect of failure is all too real and risk must be dealt with daily in the early stages of a venture. Sometimes, it's good to keep a package of Rolaids in your desk or automobile glove box. From my early experiences in jet fighters, I knew I always had a parachute and an ejection seat. I would recommend to entrepreneurs that they consider the need for a safe way to exit a disaster; be sure you bring along a "parachute." But, sometimes a safe alternative in an entrepreneurial business is just not available. Any entrepreneurial venture requires a lot of guts, but some entrepreneurial ventures take more guts than others!

Two great side benefits of entrepreneurial venturing and the assumption of risk are fun and excitement. You will most probably have a steady flow of adrenaline in your early start-up days. Ask anyone who has stepped out into a successful bold new venture to describe their experience and the words **fun** and **excitement** will show up early and often in their story. I am not talking about foolhardy or reckless behavior in embarking on a new venture, but rather a disciplined move out of your comfort zone. Any new venture will promote an ample flow of adrenaline from day-one forward.

And I personally guarantee plenty of adrenaline for you if you actually ***go start something!***

New ventures are not playgrounds for the timid, they are battlefields littered with burned-out hulks and strewn with past failures. Thankfully, there are many brilliant successes too. The failures of others must be disregarded and your highly disciplined focus must be on your own efforts if you are to succeed. You must "vision" the pot of gold awaiting you at the end of the rainbow. If you start young, and I do recommend a youthful start, you have the added benefit of being able to go bust and start all over again. Some have not succeeded until their third or fourth try. Of course, I want you to experience success on the *first* try! So be sure to use the *rules* as a checklist.

An article in a national business magazine a few years ago reported that the average age of entrepreneurs in the USA was about 40 years old. By that time in life for the average person, the kids are in college and there are a few bucks in the bank. So, by 40 it's time to start thinking about starting a business. If one has been frugal up to that point, self-capitalization of a business might be possible. That's the most desirable way to start. That guarantees that you are the owner and that you have control.

In any discussion of the *rules,* there are few concepts more important than "picking a wave," the right wave, much as Ross Perot did with computer processing services in the 1960s/70s. A well-selected wave is critical to a surfer's chance in achieving big success, of having a great surfing ride in a competition, as opposed to average success and an average ride. The choice of a good wave is helpful, perhaps necessary, to succeed in any venture. Waves in business are natural and they are plentiful. Some are more obvious than others. To succeed in a big way as an entrepreneur, it helps if you pick a good wave that is in its early stage.

There are big waves working now in the bio-tech field. Many new companies are emerging, with courageous founders surfing the giant wave they have envisioned. Some will be winners and some will be losers. Some waves are invisible to most of us but are spotted by keen-eyed entrepreneurs well in advance of their popular exploitation. Some venturers will be spectacular successes, and these will likely be the entrepreneurs who picked the best wave and are able to get on it early and ride. The basic requirements for any start-up will still be concept, courage, commitment and capital. But a good product idea and a solid business plan are assumed and required, no matter how good the wave is. Waves come in all sizes and they come rolling in continuously. Your mission: Find a good one, get on it and ride it!

One of the most incredible waves of the 20th century developed in the late '90s. It was the "dot-com" wave. In fact, the combination of eager entrepreneurs and reckless venture capitalists pushed the wave into a giant bubble. When the bubble broke early in the 21st century, the field was littered with hundreds of failed companies. But a few, those with extraordinary ideas, prospered. Two of the most successful dot-com examples are Amazon and eBay. These two companies have become basic standards of doing business in the United States and worldwide. Their growth and profitability have been phenomenal. There have been a number of other entrepreneurial start-ups to survive the dot-com disaster, but Amazon and eBay are two of the finest.

There is a good reason that I have made no comments regarding your selection of a product or service, and will not. There is no way for me, or any other person, other than you, to choose an appropriate business line to pursue. You have a unique combination of knowledge, traits and passions and those personal strengths must be the source of your business venture choice. If you're really lucky, maybe your company will be the next Amazon or eBay. More likely, if you succeed, your business will be a great source of personal wealth and satisfaction though it may not be listed on the New York Stock Exchange or NASDAQ—and that's okay. To use another baseball analogy, not everyone can bat .400 in the entrepreneurial league. But if you can bat a good solid .270, you get to play a long time and perhaps find your life's dream.

The number of business possibilities is both endless and constantly mutating. What might make a good choice today may not be such a great choice tomorrow. Many of the very best ideas, the incoming waves that will lead to new ventures, are still out of sight over the horizon. With luck and persistence, you may be the first or second to spot one of them. You might get a lead on a good idea from a close friend or confidant or you might just stumble onto a great idea yourself. There is no magic formula for picking a winning business idea. In many new ventures one can look and say, why didn't I think of that? The "obvious" is not always that obvious.

A good business idea does not necessarily need to be anything new or different. It may be that you find a better or less costly way to deliver an old product or service that yields a viable business opportunity. There is still good potential in business areas that have been around for a long time. A common trait of many successful entrepreneurial efforts in non-breakthrough products is that the entrepreneur gives a new twist and a better value to a product or service than was previously available. Deliver a better value or a better service and you may come out ahead of your competition.

For example, film processing was almost unchanged for the better part of a century. About thirty years ago a new wave of one-hour photo-processing equipment revolutionized the industry with immediate delivery of prints. One-hour processing largely replaced the old style of three- or four-day processing delay in getting your pictures back.

Now we are into the age of digital photography and the old one-hour operations have gone out of business or adapted to one-hour printing of digital files. My company shared a bit in the original move to one-hour photo processing by supplying a high-voltage power source for the electrostatic cleaning of negatives as they moved through the machines. The small wave we rode dissipated and we moved on to other products. In fact most waves eventually hit the shore and dissipate. What you hope for is a good ride while the wave lasts and the perception to go forward and spot another new wave.

The justification needed to start a successful new business might be improved value, lower cost or just an improved delivery system compared to what has been available. New market niches are abundant to the careful observer. Your access to capital will set real and unavoidable limits on your own considerations. Big ideas are hard to accomplish with little capital, yet a lot can still be done with lesser capitalization as a business develops one small step at a time.

FedEx comes to mind as an example of big success realized by adding new ideas to an old service. When Fred Smith presented his revolutionary thesis for overnight package delivery to his mentor in a graduate program, it was deemed impossible. Today, FedEx is one of the greatest corporations in the world. With great entrepreneurs, the impossible just takes a little bit longer.

There is another set of factors that may be present in the original business idea formation process of many successful ventures: Luck, chance and serendipity are frequently key in identifying a new opportunity and their importance must not be discounted. I will cover the issue of luck in greater detail later in this book. Business opportunities continue to mutate as new technology and new materials become available. The expectation of customers changes with time. All of this works to the advantage of the successful entrepreneur.

Let me emphasize that there is no time like the present to get started. A good a time to launch a new venture is ASAP. All you need is a good concept, a little capital, considerable amounts of courage and commitment, and a good measure of risk tolerance.

If you are a relatively young person, you may get several tries at a start-up. Failure is an option, not a good option, of course, but survivable. If you are middle-aged or older, then one chance may be all you will get; you can blow all your life savings and retirement money on one bad idea. Caution is critical in the selection of which, if any, venture to pursue. A well-researched, carefully reasoned and prudent decision is necessary to avoid potential disaster. Still, the path of the entrepreneur is lined with unavoidable risk.

But once the decision to start has been made, caution must be abandoned. No new start-up business succeeds that does not require an intense, fearless and all-out personal effort.

Starting a business is endless work and fun . . . plus, once in a while, as in jet aviation, there are a few moments of stark terror. I hope you will **go start something**.

A question that comes up frequently is how to name the new venture. A lot of fancy names have been conjured over the years in an effort to try to present a big and impressive façade of respectability. You have seen the adjectival concoctions of the "Advanced Hyper Nuclear Conductivity, Inc" type.

Forget all the super-cute puffy names. Put your **own name** on your company if it is your creation. There are thousands of examples where the name of the entrepreneur is the name of the company from Ford Motors to Toyota to Boeing to Dell. You may think it's egocentric but I think it's just darn good business. After all, it's your money, your guts and your hard work. There is nothing bad about the business being identified with your name.

If you are successful, you will be stunned the first time someone you meet says: "Are you *THE* Collmer of Collmer Semiconductor?" Suddenly you realize that you just might be somebody! This is a great boost to your self-esteem. Not a bad thing unless you really screw up! Then there is no place to hide. Do not worry; enough serious problems will arise to keep you from floating away with "the bighead." I think the relative advantages in personal company identification strongly support personal naming. It is always the first choice I suggest to an aspiring entrepreneur, assuming that the name is not terribly unconventional or unpronounceable.

An alternative to using your own name for the company name is to consider functional naming. Internet search engines are powerful tools and are used by many if not most purchasing personnel to find new sources of supply. Your company might be more easily found in a search if it has a functional name. One of my more recent companies, High Voltage Power Systems, had a purely functional name to make finding it on Google and other search engines a slam-dunk. Interestingly, I had gotten so much industry name identification with my self-named Collmer Semiconductor Inc., that my sales personnel had to assure customers that I was still involved in the newly named company! Still, I think we made a beneficial choice in functional naming; we received many new inquiries from the Internet as a direct result of improved searchability. In recent years, the Internet crawlers that seek out categories mentioned deeper in websites may minimize the need for functional naming.

We also discovered that advertising with an Internet search engine, such as Google, provided the option for a page-one reference and click-through to our company. We found that these positioning ads were not only very effective; they were relatively inexpensive compared with print magazine advertising. At a somewhat higher price, banner ads may be placed on all of the pages that meet the various descriptors of your product. A searcher who enters any of those descriptors for a search will likely see your ad. Ad placement on Google and other search engines can be limited to specific, small geographic market regions and may be bought for any combination of ZIP codes, states or countries. This form of advertising can be extremely effective for the start-up company.

The Internet advertising that we used was billed out on a monthly, *per-click* basis. You pay just the amount you agree to in advance for each click. A *monthly limit* for total fees can be set. Your ad is removed when the set dollar limit is reached. This system of billing for ads is very budget-friendly to a small company. This is not one of my **rules**, but it is good contemporary advice for any new business.

The best part of Internet advertising may be that you can decide to place advertisements and get nearly instant results. As a rule, small companies have small advertising budgets, so every dollar must be spent wisely. Few businesses can prosper without some kind of advertising or publicity. Internet ads are just one of many advertising venues, but the Internet is one of the best, quickest and cheapest options to consider early in your business life.

Internet ads are by far the most cost-effective medium that I have used in over forty years of product advertising. The results are almost immediate and if your site is properly designed, you will see orders from day-one. Of course, an excellent website design is essential and is assumed! There is an abundance of very talented website designers available who can be readily accessed. Website design is one area of your start-up that should not be subjected to a pinched budget.

Advertising has been the essential key for growth in all of my businesses. There is no substitute for good advertising for almost any business, local or national. In the beginning of my business efforts at Varo, I was working in the pre-Internet era and the ads were never aimed as accurately as the Internet allows now.

A well-designed website has become a fundamental requirement for almost any business, large or small. Potential customers see so many excellent sites that you may be misjudged based on the adequacy of your site if it is sub-standard. If you accept orders on your site, the site must be customer-friendly. We have all had the experience of visiting sites that were so opaque that they actually resisted customers! So once again, do not be overly tight in approving website design expenses.

There are a myriad of concerns for the entrepreneur moving into his/her first new business venture. There is no way that all of the issues that the entrepreneur will face can be anticipated. Maintaining a positive attitude in dealing with issues as they arise will usually carry the day.

Finally, I would like to repeat: The biggest issues for you to deal with from a personal point of view are concept, courage, commitment, capital and risk. No successful business emerges unless the founders recognize and acknowledge these factors.

CHAPTER 4

NO PARTNERSHIPS!

If you decide to be involved in a partnership, your risk in starting a new enterprise grows dramatically. The reason is that partnerships are inherently unstable.

Perhaps the most important of the 50 **rules** is to never do a 50/50 partnership; they are inherently unstable. The "No Partnership" rule is critical to your long-term mental and financial health. I will discuss the problems inherent in partnerships in this chapter and why you need to avoid partnerships at almost any cost. We will look at both silent financial partners and actual participating partners. One of the most important elements of this discussion is that you should never put yourself into either a 50/50 ownership position or in a minority ownership position if you are planning a long-term involvement.

If you do get into a partnership, it should be only for the purpose of satisfying short-range goals to gain the financial resources needed to make the next step to success, success being defined as actually controlling your own company, that is, more than 50% ownership. If you violate this rule and have lasting success, you will have achieved success in a low-probability environment. Most 50/50 partnerships and minority-position ownerships may result in extreme agony for you, the non-controlling partner.

Financial partners are the folks with the gold that you may need to start a business. They can be very persuasive and convince you that your 30-40% ownership is actually a good thing. In some cases they may be right. They may say that they have no plans to co-opt your management position, so just relax. If they do not want to run the company, and if they really mean that and stick to it, your minority position may never be a problem.

But beware: Your minority ownership will more likely be a problem at some point if you want sanity in your life. Minority ownership means you can be pushed around or pushed out by the controlling interest for almost any reason. Of course, good legal work upfront can help minimize that threat. But the majority financial investor almost always has control of all business decisions if he so chooses. The main reason that minority positions concern me is investor greed. If your new venture is successful, you may find the investor's son-in-law running "your" business. I cannot stress this point enough. ***The main reason to be an entrepreneur is to set your own course and be the master of your domain.*** A minority position or a 50/50 position almost guarantees that you will not be able to do that. Again, in my opinion, the only good reason to be in a minority position is to generate a big enough stake to start your own business later.

50/50 "sweat equity" partners are another big trap. You put up the money and effort and they put up just their effort as their share in the new business venture. While they may not behave as an equal partner early in the business, with success they are likely to assert their 50% position. I have witnessed too many ventures that have broken up due to battles between equal partners.

As George Orwell wrote in his seminal novel *Animal Farm,* some animals become "more equal than others." In a partnership, one of the partners will eventually become "more equal." It's just human nature to see oneself wearing a white hat, and the other guy, the partner, no matter how beloved in the past, wearing a black hat.

I don't have quantitative data, but the number of breakups that I have witnessed is amazing. In today's marriages, where the modern man and woman have a 50/50 relationship, 55% end up divorced. I suspect that an even greater break-up percentage applies to business partnerships.

Be the owner or be the employee. In the event of a serious disagreement, if you are an employee, you can decide to leave and go elsewhere. If you're a 50% owner or a minority owner you cannot just walk away. In any business someone has to be in charge and be able to make final decisions. The worst frustration in the world is the tugging that is inevitable between two equal partners on differences of opinion regarding business risks and business opportunities. There are few good entrepreneurs who will agree all the time with anyone else. It may just be a tiny difference to start, but once friction ignites, it tends to grow rapidly. Just as in failing marriages, every kind of minor issue becomes a part of the bigger war. Frequently, the business staggers under the load of controversy and then disintegrates, with both parties being losers.

Fathers who leave their business to two or more children have no idea of the coming havoc they may be creating as sibling rivalry raises its ugly head a few years down the road. This is especially true if serious amounts of money are involved. You do not need a lot of business experience to have witnessed the incredible mess siblings can make in each other's lives and in their families. Further, the result of such fights frequently has a destructive impact on the business.

The same issues exist in nearly all partnerships; witness the continual fragmenting of law and accounting partnerships. Some enlightened partnerships give management authority to just one person and the other partners live by the decisions made. If the "managing partner" is enlightened, he will resist making large decisions without a full hearing of the other partner's opinions. Consensus is the desired outcome but it isn't always possible.

Long-term consensus is rare and is not the usual outcome, whether in a business or in a marriage.

If you just have to be in a 50/50 partnership, you will need the services of a very competent lawyer to construct a bullet-proof "buy-sell" agreement. With such an agreement, if divorce becomes inevitable in the partnership, the rules of separation are clearly stated in advance. The most common arrangement is that either partner can offer to buy the other out for a specified offering price. The other partner then has the option to either buy or sell from the challenging partner at the offered price.

There are other details such as non-compete clauses or pre-agreed terms in addition to the buy-sell agreement. A good lawyer will have a load of suggestions to pick from as the agreement is put together. You want to be sure you and your partner have full audit rights at any time and guaranteed access to the financial and personnel books of the business. An annual audit by a competent, independent CPA is a good idea. This is true for even a relatively small private business partnership. Access to all relevant tax documents by all partners must be guaranteed since you will all have to sign them. Just a reminder: You or your partner's failure to pay Federal Income Tax withholding and FICA taxes for your employees in a timely manner can lead to IRS hell and possibly to a criminal action and jail-time!

No matter how close or enduring the friendship with your partner may be at the beginning of a venture, there must be a solid contract on the manner in which to dissolve the partnership in the event of irresolvable dispute, illness or death. That agreement must be signed and sealed before the first dollar is invested. Don't make the huge mistake of going on faith.

I think that the only thing worse than a 50/50 owner-operated partnership is a minority interest in an entrepreneurial venture. If you make a cash investment in the ownership of the venture, but you are in a minority position, your money is locked up for eternity; at least it will seem like an eternity. Minority ownership in a small company dominated by a majority owner may lead to destructive results on your psyche. If you can get a carried interest (free ownership or stock options), you might be OK if your expectations are low, or if lightning strikes and the venture takes off like a rocket ship and ends up being sold to the public for a large multiple in an Initial Public Offering (IPO). The odds do not favor a grand outcome. But they do happen! Check out Facebook!

If the business outcome is just average or worse, your interest is essentially frozen and your input on key decisions may be totally ignored. What can you do? You're stuck. Your money, your future, your reputation and maybe your incredible contribution to the success of the enterprise are handcuffed and the majority owner has the keys. If you are just an employee (with a high salary and perhaps a cost-free stock option), you can walk away at any time. I think that is better than a minority investment position by a mile!

Be the boss or be the employee . . . everything in-between is not very attractive unless you get really lucky. I would hate to see you depend purely on luck (but, more about luck later).

Ronald Reagan said about arms treaties with the old USSR: "Trust, but verify." That should be your rule in dealing with a partner: Trust but verify!

The rule is NO 50/50 partnerships, ever. Trust me on this!

GOAL SETTING

When discussing the rules for the entrepreneur, one of the most important is goal setting. Most successful people set personal goals for long, medium and short range periods. Goal setting is always critical to success. Before an entrepreneurial business start-up commences, goals must be carefully set and a comprehensive business plan put into writing.

Your dreams, goals and vision must come first. If there is no clearly stated, overall purpose and desired result for what you are planning, then there is no significant framework to guide your detailed business planning and the onrush of decision-making.

The four goals that I set for myself after leaving Varo in 1978 became my new set of "life goals." These new goals were not just ordinary business goals but required a successful business venture to bring them to fulfillment. You might call these overarching goals a vision or even a dream. Dreaming is essential to all of us so that our emotions get aligned with our more objective business-oriented thinking. Until you have a dream you have not yet reached the peak of your potential.

I have continued to make detailed written goals every year of my business life. I have not accomplished all of them or even most of them. Some of my goals have been amended from time to time. But goals, once set, tend to take on a life of their own and push us toward success. This book is the fulfillment of one of my written goals. It stems from the list of entrepreneurial **rules** that I developed during visits to MBA classes over the last 20 years.

Dreams do not have to be realistic but their very existence might make their realization possible. Dreams move us to achieve results that are seemingly impossible. Chasing a dream may lead to a serendipitous discovery; in the process of chasing one dream, another may leap out in front of you. Goals should not inhibit you from grabbing an opportunity that just appears out of the mist! Goals are subject to amendment, but written goals must be set nevertheless so that you have a frame of reference to evaluate pop-up opportunities.

Goal setting is the first big step to getting your life and your business in order. You should get into the habit of writing your goals for the long term, intermediate term and most importantly, the short term: one year or even one month. If you just think about your goals and fail to write them down, the effort is wasted. Once you have written a goal, the chances of achieving it are multiplied dramatically. The act of writing goals forces critical choices and focuses your thinking. You will find that goal prioritization happens almost automatically once the ideas hit paper or the computer. Prioritization is a critical process since it becomes obvious that you probably can't achieve everything on your list. Choices must be made.

The long-term goals that you set—say, five years—will help focus the lesser periods of one, two or three years. But even if all you do in goal setting is to set one-year goals, you will get most of the benefits of written goals. Every short-term goal should lead to a "next step" that leads unambiguously toward the achievement of your long-term goals. The key question to ask after setting a goal is: "what will I do tomorrow and next week to move a step closer to achievement of this goal?" If a clear next step is not in sight, the goal is just fantasy and you are wasting valuable time. Stick with realistic yet stretchy goals.

Your one-year goals should not be set at such a level of difficulty that they are likely to fail. Your goals should be very specific and contain a time frame for achievement. The primary purpose of annual goals and even shorter term goals is to help you develop an orderly process that clearly and concisely leads you toward the achievement of your longer term goals. The longer term goals, especially five years or longer, may not in themselves yield a clear path toward achievement. That's OK. The further out the time scale of the goal, the more speculative it becomes and the goal begins to take on the characteristics of a dream. The clear focus has to be on the one-year goal horizon and the clearly defined "next steps."

Of course, when very large capitalizations are involved, long-range planning may have longer horizons extending to or beyond one or more decades. In this book, I am mostly considering the smaller entrepreneur, the first-time start-up entrepreneur, to whom one- to five-year goals will be more significant.

Almost all great achievement begins with a dream, from Columbus's dream of a new route to India to Ray Kroc's dream of a better way to serve the humble hamburger and fries. I guess it would be possible to simply have a dream of wealth, but I doubt that there are many clear, concrete "next steps" forward that might be stimulated by that dream. Still, dreams are critically important. You must remember that your customers' delight will be your key to success. The best dreams are those that illuminate a path that leads to better lives for others. The actual path toward your achievement may be through the invention of new products or services or simple concepts for better efficiencies in manufacturing, distribution or marketing. But, there is rarely a big success without a big dream first.

I would like to note that goals are not immutable. Room should be left in your thinking for opportunistic changes, or "serendipity."

Columbus did not find a new route to India. But he did discover a new world! Almost certainly, serendipity will be a factor in your business life, too, so you need to allow for it. Goals are not a straitjacket! Goals are your best guide for success, but the path may need to shift from time to time to accommodate new thinking and new circumstances.

On the other hand, paraphrasing G. K. Chesterton, if your mind is *too* open, your brains might fall out!

In football, the goal line is clearly identified with a very bright white line. The ball needs only to break the plane of the goal line in order to count as a touchdown. The hundred-yard path from the opposite end of the field is marked in one-, five-and ten-yard increments. The steps to get to the goal line are clear; there are 99 steps, 99 yards to get there.

Like football, where the goal line is clear and marked with chalk, would-be entrepreneurs must also have clear-cut goals in their business life as well as in their personal life. You, the entrepreneur, must also have a mental picture of what the goal line looks like. You cannot score if you do not know which direction leads to the goal. Goal setting is not magic, but it comes close. Just the exercise of setting, writing and prioritizing goals is a major step forward. You may change your mind later—no problem, that may be a healthy move—but you must have goals!

Remember, if the goals are not written, they do not count. You might hear people say, "I know what my goals are; I do not need to write them down." Once again, if the goals are not written, they are not really goals.

There should be a golden rule that reads:

No goals, no gold.

If readers get only one thing from this book, it should be that he/she must have written goals.

That, and no partnerships: never, never! These two *rules* are the guts of this book.

You must develop and write your goals every year and you must review them periodically. Make several copies of your goals and put them in places where you will stumble over them. There is no need to be rigid about it, but frequent review does no harm and might lead to deeper insights.

Real goals must be written!

When you set your one-year goals, you must see a well-defined path for achievement. The question you should never forget to ask yourself is: "What is the **next step** that I can take right now to advance toward my ultimate goal?" Still, if you do nothing more than make a written list of your goals, you will have made a major improvement in your chances for success.

As you approach the end of every year, sit down, take a look at your ending year's goals, then stop, think carefully, and start writing your goals for the coming year. Be sure to carefully review and score your written goals from the past year, before writing new ones. I hope your goal-setting efforts never result in your just changing the date on last year's goals! Once you have completed your new goals, you may or may not refer to them as the year goes by, but the fact that you have written them down will etch them in your mind and make them real.

When you review your annual goals, you can check off the goals you hit and mark the goals you missed. On the goals you missed, try to explain to yourself why you missed a goal. Five-year goals work the same way. Those goals give you a target to shoot at. Ten-year goals give you an even bigger, broader target.

If you want to achieve wealth, every goal should be written down as a short- or long-term goal. If you want to achieve fame, that should be written down, too. If you want to serve humanity, that should be written down. Most of these personal goals cannot be achieved without first achieving significant wealth. You cannot be a philanthropist without big bucks.

Each of your goals should have enough specificity and a clear time frame so that progress against the goals can be periodically assessed, especially the one-year goals. You need to have some idea in broad terms as to how you might actually achieve the goal if it's a five-year goal or even a ten-year goal. Still, reality is a key aspect in goal setting. Keep it real.

The "why" question should be asked for each and every goal not met. If you decide to re-set a missed goal, then the question is: What is the next step to its achievement? That's also a question that you should ask at the end of every business planning meeting, **what's the next step.** Until you have clearly identified the next step, any goal continues to recede into the future. Any business meeting without a next step or do-list will have been a waste of time. You must have next steps in order to make progress. The next steps end up being your operational battle plan, your tactical plan, the plan for what tasks you actually intend to get done today that lead to where you want to be tomorrow.

Since even the best business plan can fail, I have always gone one step beyond fundamental business planning and budgeting to develop and maintain informal contingency plans. A contingency plan is fundamentally an escape plan for unexpected disasters. As I mentioned before, I was a military jet pilot and I always had to wear a parachute and sat in an ejection seat . . . so, that's the kind of contingency I'm talking about, a figurative ejection seat and parachute. Good goal setting should include your personal parachute!

In an entrepreneurial start-up, your own habits and personality can be the biggest issue leading to success or failure. If you have missed your goals, you may be the problem, but with luck you can modify your own behavior and become part of the solution. Until you identify your problems and lay them out in the form of future goals to be achieved, you have not done your job, and your chances of big success are thereby reduced. Many people focus on their weaknesses, striving for improvement in those areas. I think it is a better policy to focus on your strengths and run them as hard as you can. Let your strengths lead you. Try to keep your weaknesses from shackling you. You may not be able to eliminate them, but at least try to minimize them.

I began writing annual goals as a young man early in my employment career. The goals were not very elegant at the start but they grew better as time went by. My employer decided to be more formal and adopted an incentive plan based on goal setting and accomplishment. The incentive plan payments were attached to the achievement of specific goals. In my opinion, goal-based individual incentive plans are not a particularly good system, because the plan tends to force you to establish goals that you believe you can achieve easily. That's sandbagging, and sandbagging is bad, and is very difficult for management to detect in advance. Your personal goals should be set so that you need to stretch to accomplish them. You need them to stretch you. But, if you are human, you don't want missed goals to adversely affect your income. If you are going to lose money with over-ambitious goals, good judgment demands a bit of sandbagging!

I have always felt that there are only two kinds of companies in regard to goal-based incentive plans: companies that want to get into incentive plans and companies that want to get out of incentive plans. The principal benefits of goal setting do not require incentive plans for their power. Goals are powerful in themselves because they give the goal-setter a clear and unambiguous approach to dealing with reality. Goals provide ongoing prompts that will generate improvements in performance for both you and your subordinates'. As an entrepreneur, you need not necessarily share your goals with anyone else. Just the fact that you have written goals will drive your performance and your associates will follow your leadership if they think you have a clear vision and plan.

Goal setting is not an easy process and it's not a natural process. Our natural tendency is to procrastinate. Goal setting is just the opposite of that. Goals are not always obvious. Well-set goals require a considerable amount of critical thought and prioritization. Times change, we change, and our goals can change too. As I mentioned earlier, goal setting should not be so rigorous that it does not allow for active and rapidly shifting environments in which we can change our minds and modify our course based on the opportunities that we meet. Being overly rigid can be a problem in itself.

Goal setting, planning and budgeting should always allow for opportunistic developments. If you were heading down a road and you suddenly discovered the bridge in front of you was out, you would stop. All planning has to be done on that same basis; if the bridge is out, stop! When the goal becomes unattainable or unreasonable or undesirable, you must be willing to change it.

Still, the golden rule applies: **No goals, no gold.**

One of the most incredible goal-setting exercises in the 20th century was when John Kennedy set the goal in 1961 of putting a man on the moon before the end of the decade of the 1960s. In fact, Neil Armstrong stepped off the Apollo 11 Lunar Module on July 20, 1969. If President Kennedy had not set that goal, the odds of an American landing on the moon probably would have been very low. Landing on the moon may or may not have been a particularly desirable objective from a practical and financial point of view, but it was a huge political, technological and scientific accomplishment.

I'll have to admit that when I heard John Kennedy set the goal of going to the moon, I really thought that it was an unattainable goal that would lead to an embarrassing failure. So sometimes, when we set a goal that seems too far out for us to actually reach, we can do far more than we thought we could do. Most goals need to be attainable with less than the superhuman effort generated to put a man on the moon. Still, dreaming is encouraged!

When you make the decision to actually sit down and write your own goals, you must be painfully realistic. Goals that have no chance for success should never be set. Goals should be a stretch, there's no question about that, but they should also be realistic and have some chance of attainability. Setting lofty goals and never achieving them is very demoralizing, and you could eventually decide that goal setting is a waste of time. So goals must be realistic.

The key to well-set goals is that the goals should have obvious steps to achievement. As I have mentioned before, "What is the next step?" The best goals always have a next step. If a next step is not obvious, re-think the goal; it may be too much of a stretch.

An annual goal-setting session is the single best habit that you can develop as an entrepreneur and as a manager. The management of some companies goes on a two- or three-day retreat for no other purpose.

Strategy, planning and budgeting are the holy grail of management training. I certainly don't want to be dismissive of these concepts and practices. They are very essential, especially in very large operations. However, while the entrepreneur must set his goals and have a plan, you must be careful to avoid the old truism of "paralysis by analysis."

A friend of mine is an engineer for a large corporation that has a very extensive strategy and planning practice. Each significant individual in the company generates a highly detailed planning document that extends over a period of a year and perhaps beyond. I was discussing my friend's work with him and he told me about a significant cost-reducing idea that he had. I asked him whether it would be implemented soon. He said no, he could not bring it up, since he had just finished writing his planning manual and that if he offered some change to it, it would be looked upon poorly by management. Further, since the bureaucracy would make it almost impossible to make the change, he would suppress the idea until the next annual planning cycle.

I have no doubt that the elegant system used by his company produced extraordinary results. However, it apparently cut off access to new ideas and creative innovation that might have been applied in a timely manner had not the corporate goal amending system been so complex. It is somewhat ironic that this same company professes to be one of the seats of high-tech innovation in the world. A healthy balance of stability and an allowance for change in goal setting probably works best.

The Japanese have avoided some of these idea gridlocks by installing bottom-up management. Of course the Japanese system is not completely bottom-up, but new ideas are accessed immediately to generate improvements in company performance and especially in quality control.

As an entrepreneur you must be capable of recognizing significant opportunities and have enough flexibility in your planning and budgeting to take advantage of them. Keep your mind open for ideas coming from the outside or from the inside. Within the entrepreneurial sphere, it is very easy to make running changes since very few people, perhaps only one, you, are involved in the decision-making process.

On the other hand, continually and capriciously changing course and priorities can cause a total disruption of an operation and eventual failure. Every quail hunter knows that if you have a bird dog that quits pointing out quail and starts chasing rabbits, you shoot him. I have used the chasing rabbits analogy to describe efforts that are off the established track. One must be careful to distinguish between a truly new and better opportunity and just another rabbit to be chased. All of your energy and resources could be easily wasted if you don't stick reasonably close to your plans, goals and objectives.

When I started my own company, I had a particular affinity for a product line that I knew very well and that I had had customer experience with in the past. My goals were pretty much set along the lines of that class of products. The supplier company, a large Japanese concern, came out with a whole new approach, with a different set of new products not directly related to what I had been initially interested in. Fortunately, we recognized that opportunity, shifted gears and moved in a different direction. We succeeded in building a relatively large business based mostly on the new opportunity. We did not forsake the original product concept or the customers associated with it and continued to use that as a base to stand on and the new approach provided a great opportunity for the expansion of my company.

A final goal-setting tip: Have a printer make up some 2.75" x 4.5" cards for your shirt pocket. The corners of the cards should be rounded so they won't easily dog-ear when carried in your pocket. Print your company name and contact data on the bottom edge of the card. You can put a highly screened, barely visible logo in the center of the card. Always carry a supply of note cards in your pocket. Write your daily and/or weekly goals and tasks on these cards. I know how effective computerized calendars and schedules are, but you can't beat pocket cards. You can make notes and changes as you go.

I think pocket cards may be better than a PDA, computer or iPhone/iPad. Plus, when you're done with the cards you can put them in a file for possible future reference. Of course you can log your notes onto your computer and/or your iPhone, iPad, Android, Blackberry or PDA. But, I have found pocket cards to be the most helpful management aid that I have ever used. You can also use these cards in lieu of a business card. If they're done well they can be quite attractive. Think color; the card does not necessarily need to be done in black and white.

As new technological advances have been made in phones and computers, I have tried to be an early adopter. I certainly recognize the incredible capability of both the portable and desktop computers and phones. So, the pocket cards may be a little dinosaurian, but they absolutely work . . . even when the battery fails!

There are few more valuable habits in life or in any kind of business than setting personal and business goals. Be a goal setter and go for the gold.

SAVE 10%

If you're planning to be an entrepreneur, start saving 10% "off the top" today. Otherwise you'll always be working for someone else and fattening their account. In my view, an entrepreneur must have most of his own starting capital. In addition to your start-up-capital, you will need at least two years personal expense reserve in the bank if you plan to do a start-up.

Bottom line: If you wish to be a capitalist, you've got to have capital.

There is no substitute for adequate capital in a start-up. Would-be entrepreneurs frequently see great start-up opportunities but have little or no capital to take advantage of them. If Other People's Money (OPM) is needed to get the enterprise started, and if it is successful, the business may eventually belong to the "Other People." This could defeat the very purpose of starting your own business. If you must use OPM, keep the investor in a minority ownership position. I will do another section on the importance of *control*, that is, maintaining at least 51% ownership of your company's voting stock.

There is another Golden Rule in business, especially appropriate to start-ups:

He who has the gold makes the rules.

If you do need, and then find a financial backer, which is no small task, and he puts up a majority of the capital needed to start your business, if you are successful, you may end up reporting to a boss. This is not what you intended when you decided to go start something. You will be wondering how he could ignore all the good things he told you and the promises about his good intentions when he originally invested. If you are really successful, he might very well just try to throw you out. Financial partners can be very traitorous if they are majority equity holders.

The venture capital industry does some wonderful things but you cannot absolutely rely on unwritten promises. Sharks swim in those waters. As a beginning entrepreneur you may make very attractive shark food! I don't want to say that outside investment can't be done successfully, but you must look at every aspect of the deal and look very carefully at every detail of the investment agreement to avoid a surprise. A good lawyer is indispensable. Any truly good deal should be able to survive legal scrutiny.

The most frequent cause of failure in start-ups is under-capitalization. Good planning can minimize the problem, but it seems that almost every start-up project takes longer and costs more than originally planned. There is little sympathy for the entrepreneur who runs out of money before the project gets off the ground. If you run out of money, new capital will come at a very high price. Almost certainly you will lose control of your business. So, careful capital planning is an important issue for any business and especially for a start-up. Most projects generally cost substantially more than the original estimate and take twice the estimated time to complete. But you'd better believe that overrunning your estimated start-up costs and time schedules can be a real problem for the thinly capitalized entrepreneur. When your original money is gone, you may find yourself at the mercy of the sharks.

The best and primary source for initial starting capital for a new business, other than your own personal funds, is known as "angel money." It is the money that you can secure from investors who don't demand a controlling position as a condition of investment. If you use only your own money, the business will absolutely belong to you, no questions asked! Banks rarely loan any of the initial start-up capital needed for founding a new venture. Banks need assets to lend against: collateral! Even then, banks usually will loan only a fractional amount of your assets' value.

At the end of the last century, in the late 1990s, public money became available for the hot "dot-coms," the dawning of the true Internet Age. Embryonic companies started with an IPO, public money, based on nothing more than a paper plan and a thin promise In those brief "good old days" of the Internet bubble, money was very, very loose. But those days are gone now, perhaps forever. You may have your feelings hurt if you expect a big welcome at the bank or with an investment banker when you try to approach them for seed money.

The best and, well, the old-fashioned way to access capital is to inherit it. If you are like me, that was just not an option. Occasionally, a personal loan from a family member can be the initial stake you need to get going. Family money can be fickle though, and you may eventually regret the problems that inevitably go with family money and the resulting family involvement. I guess some individuals might welcome the opportunity to involve extended family in the ownership of your business. I did not want to do that in my own case and it was not practical for me and my family anyhow.

Family money does increase your risk for being able to maintain control of critical decision-making. I think family money has far too many strings attached to be attractive. If things go badly, you will have a lifetime of recriminations. Christmas will be no fun at all! If your money comes from your in-laws . . . God bless you. Life will never be the same. I think most of the best reasons to go start something will be destroyed!

If you are relatively young, I recommend that you adopt a serious personal savings plan that will eventually provide you with that ever-so-valuable starting seed-capital money. If you set aside 10% of your earnings, preferably before tax, you will begin to accumulate that vital nest egg. Since the average starting entrepreneur in America is about 40 years old, you should plan to accumulate a respectable bank account by the time you reach that age. I hope you can get rolling long before then. But no matter when you get started; it will be very helpful to have accumulated as much personal capital as possible, so that you are not forced to rely on other sources for equity financing. I remember a number of friends whose goals were to be a millionaire before the age of 40. Some did achieve that. I never had that as a goal but accomplished it anyhow. I hope you can do the same!

When I was 12 years old, an older friend of the family told me the reasons why I should save 10% of every dime I ever earned. He understood the need for a rainy-day fund as well as a source of funds to invest. I wasn't able to do that 100% of the time, but I did it as well as I could. Personal savings were then and are now the single best source of start-up money for the small entrepreneurial venture. The benefit of slavish saving is that when an opportunity does come along, you actually have some cash to take advantage of it. The best investment opportunity in the world is virtually worthless to you if you don't have any money in the bank. If you want to be a capitalist, you've got to have capital, and savings is the primary path available to most of us.

In my early and very humble employment immediately after leaving the Navy, my wife and I still managed to save 10% of my paycheck by having the money deducted and automatically deposited to a credit union account. There were many days when the temptation to raid this account was almost overpowering, but we resisted. It was very difficult to resist tapping those funds, since we had three young children and we were compelled to budget our expenses down to the last penny. There were dozens of times in any year when a few extra bucks would have come in handy. We stuck to our savings plan even with no clear objective in sight. Starting a business was certainly not a part of our family plan early on; we just felt the need for a rainy-day fund.

I'm glad I had been urged to save that 10% early in my adolescence. I am deeply indebted to the great family friend, Jack Reich, who was a senior executive at Sears in Dallas. He had the right idea. I am also indebted for the financial diligence and patience of my wife, Suzanne. She was willing to hold the line on expenses, difficult as it was. Saving is never fun for young families but it is an important habit necessary for future success. I am passing Jack Reich's advice on to you! Believe it! Set up a strong savings plan for you and your family.

Our savings fund wasn't huge when an opportunity popped up to make a significant investment in my employer, Varo Inc. Varo was a publicly-traded company with its stock listed on the American Stock Exchange at that time. Varo became essentially insolvent in 1970, but the banks decided to take it over and do a workout. That was actually a good thing for me, as my tiny division was profitable and growing. My division was spun off, becoming Varo Semiconductor Inc., and our stock was held as collateral at the bank. The bank let the newly formed Semiconductor company operate semi-autonomously. I was made president and chairman of the newly created entity. Over a period of five years our little division grew rapidly, with very strong profitability.

The balance of the company, with bank-appointed management, made slow progress after selling or shutting down a dozen losing operations. In order to inject capital, the banks took a significant stock position in the parent company. As we began to see a bit of daylight, the owning banks offered to sell some of their stock to management as a motivational tool. Since my wife and I had a bit of capital saved up by then, I was able to participate in acquisition of bank stock and acquire yet more stock on the public market.

Incidentally, Varo's stock was trading on the American Stock Exchange at approximately one-times earnings! No one noticed that the company was making progress, even though our news releases clearly stated the improved situation. The stock market players had totally abandoned the company as it had become a market pariah during the near insolvency. My wife and I bought outright as much stock as we could afford. We were able to increase the number of stock shares we purchased by borrowing funds from the stock-owning bank and thereby taking on significant leverage, always scary!

I do not necessarily recommend leverage to everyone since it can lead to really big problems. Witness the widespread destruction of financial institutions in 2009 due primarily to highly leveraged investment positions. You must be extra careful when you use any leverage! Leverage is a very sharp knife that cuts both ways. Still, leverage can multiply a win handsomely. It seems to me that more people prosper from leverage than not, especially in small business start-ups. A friend of mine in the real estate business whom I mentioned earlier had told me once before that a dollar borrowed was a dollar earned and a dollar paid back was a dollar lost forever! I will not go that far in a defense of leverage, but leverage must still be an agenda item to be considered as your business progresses.

The Varo stock purchase was a "bet the farm" opportunity for my wife and me. The company was in a difficult turnaround situation but we could see that there was a good chance of survival with progress being made daily. There was full disclosure to the public, but once investors are burned by a stock, there is little market interest in it as it comes back from the brink. I could also see that my own personal efforts were going to be crucial to the company's emergence from virtual insolvency and that the return for the investment might be substantial if we succeeded. We did, and it was!

By 1976, we were able to merge the two Varo companies—Varo Inc., the parent, and Varo Semiconductor Inc.,—market the bank stock and get a listing on the New York Stock Exchange. I became president of the parent at that time.

Had my wife and I not carefully saved for many years, the opportunity would have just passed us by. As it happened, that chance to substantially multiply our savings gave us the chance to start our own company a few years later. Once again, there is no substitute for the accumulation of even a small amount of personal capital if you want to be an entrepreneur.

Growing your savings account through careful investment is certainly helpful. With a little luck your investments can be decisive in the accumulation of enough capital for a true entrepreneurial business start-up. It may take you a couple of steps up the capital ladder to get sufficient accumulated funds for a personally-owned enterprise, but the effort is well worth it.

I have made capital accumulation rule one of the first ten **rules** because without successfully accumulating capital to fund a start-up, the rest of the **rules** are almost meaningless. You must have enough capital to get started. If you are to be successful, and you have significant retained earnings, you may not be forced to sacrifice control of the business in order to raise the additional funding needed to grow your business. That's where a good banking relationship may come in handy. Financing receivables and inventories, and even some capital assets, through a bank usually does not mean that you have to give up control. Bank borrowing may be difficult, but it should be carefully investigated as a good alternative to equity investments by outsiders.

I want to emphasize that the most important key to a successful start-up is to avoid the trap of cash starvation. A great business starved for cash makes a tasty target for a predator. There is no doubt that adequate up-front capitalization is a must for the entrepreneur.

Either you eat the bear or the bear eats you!

Once you have decided to go into a start-up venture, availability of capital without too many strings attached becomes critically important. Without capital there can be no venture. And, until the deal is completely understood, no one can finally determine the amount of capital required. For the sake of this discussion, I will stipulate that the amount must simply be . . . enough.

While banks and venture capitalists are rarely the source of money for a venture start-up, that does not mean you should not try. Additionally, there are numerous "angel funds" around that will put limited investments into a fledgling effort, but your business plan has to be really good. If there is the potential for your loss of a controlling interest in the voting stock, your appetite for angel money may be dulled. In my opinion, you should walk away if sacrificing majority ownership interest to the investor is one of the terms for getting the money. Even a dull job in a factory or office is better than a bad venture. You might contact a nearby graduate management school whose programs frequently have access to angel money sources in your region. Asking is free of charge!

In your search for starting capital, you might find individuals with more money than sense who are willing to make a loose bet on your eventual success and are willing to take a minority ownership position. You must defend your 51%-plus ownership in any deal you make for capital. This is a critical point. Again, a good lawyer is indispensable to a successful input of outside capital investment.

You will find that banks lend money mostly against assets. You might find a bank or "third party" financing (GE Capital for example) to provide purchase money necessary for large equipment, assuming you put up a down payment and the equipment is readily resalable in case of your default. Another avenue is the possibility of leasing needed facilities and equipment from the owners. Your personal creditworthiness will be an issue in all of these venues. Most lenders will require a personal guarantee and evidence of collateral to back the guarantee. To some extent, the ease of the terms and conditions by which equipment can be leased are determined by the excess availability of the equipment sought. For example, in recent years, it has been relatively easy to start a new airline, since there were many older aircraft available for leasing.

Venture capitalists (VC), in order to make a substantial investment, usually want to see a business start-up that is already successful and making a strong move on its own money but needs more investment input to really grow. This is sometimes referred to as *mezzanine financing*. There are many factors in a VC decision to invest in your enterprise, but your management team, ongoing success, strong potential for profitability, and a clear multi-year plan are essential. Still, you need to maintain 51% control in any deal. That may be difficult to do, but your efforts will be rewarded if you are successful.

As I mentioned earlier, during the boom years of the late '90s, the dot-com ventures got started with little or no market experience, no profits and no operations. They sometimes secured huge amounts of venture capital, and in some cases actually did large Initial Public Offerings (IPOs) on a wing and a prayer with nothing but a hyped business plan. Incredibly, many of these start-ups made an initial public offering to raise their angel money! Those days flowered and withered in a very short period of time. Many overly eager investors lost a lot of money. Many of those projects were ill-conceived, and contributed to the giant dot-com bubble that eventually burst in the early 2000s, with great damage to equity markets generally. There is no way anyone can count on public market sources for money in today's new ventures.

Today it takes a solid business plan with a high probability of success to interest outside investors. You may have enough confidence in your ability to proceed with your own money. If you are successful in turning your enterprise into a profitable business, even if relatively small, mezzanine financing and bank money may become more available.

I repeat, one of the main causes of failure in new ventures is shortage of capital. You simply can't run without money. Cash flow gets out of hand very easily in a new venture and your treasury can become broken. This issue puts a tremendous premium on cash planning at the outset. One must not only provide for the venture money needed but also the cash needed for one's own livelihood. A working spouse is a great help in a small venture where every penny counts. The best rule is to have the money saved up and available before you consider starting a new business venture.

I remember in the early days of starting my own electronics business in 1979, we advertised nationally, acquired national sales representatives and eagerly sought new customers. One young fellow saw our direct-mail ad and called from Boston with his special electronic component requirements. We knew he was calling from his family kitchen because we could hear the baby and the dog in the background. This does not normally make for a very stable, creditworthy customer for a fledgling venture such as ours to invest in.

Nevertheless, though we had very limited cash, we had the product he needed, and we decided to bet on him because of his engineering brilliance. We extended him credit, sold him parts for his initial designs and over a few years he built a stunningly large company. We remained a major supplier for a number of years. We were only a couple of steps ahead of him as entrepreneurs, so we could identify with his issues, and both of us got lucky.

So, businesses can get started at the kitchen table and can be financed with the help of suppliers who will extend credit. But the new company must also have some capital to stand on. Before he made his start-up attempt, this young engineer had earned some money, saved it very carefully and thus had the opportunity to actually do a fresh start-up. Over a very few years he built a highly successful business that was eventually sold for enough for him to retire in style. There are hundreds of thousands of successful new ventures throughout America every year. I hope you are able to go start one.

The small-business boom in America is nothing new. It's been around for two centuries. The thing that has made America great has been our broad ability to innovate and to start businesses in market sectors where larger interests don't even want to participate. Large businesses frequently have huge blind spots when it comes to new markets.

The best thing about a new venture is that it is new!

A new venture may not involve high technology or other new high-tech developments, but it will by its nature be a new approach to doing business. Some of the late 20th-century start-ups have become mainline New York Stock Exchange/NASDAQ favorites today; Microsoft, Dell, Amazon and eBay are great examples.

I repeat once more, I will make no attempt in this book to tell you what kind of business you should start, what scale you should try to start on, or how much capital you might need to get started. I will tell you that you must consider the role of capital in what you are trying to do. But be absolutely sure you have enough to avoid an early and sudden business death or the loss of your efforts to a predator.

There are a variety of ways to raise personal capital. One of the paths to eventual personal financial success is to be part of a start-up venture early in your career with minority equity participation. Perhaps you might make enough money to do a second venture later in which you are the majority investor. I have witnessed many examples of this two-step approach to business formation. That was certainly the approach that I took, although that was not my intention. In fact, I have seen a couple of entrepreneurs go three steps to final full ownership and control. In each step the entrepreneur had accumulated a bit more capital and gained a larger measure of ownership and finally became financially able to control his or her own business.

That word *control* is a very critical concept. If you own less than 50% you may think you have control because of your technical knowledge or your business ability, but you really do not have *control.* Fifty-one percent of the voting stock in the company is a minimum number for certain control of any start-up venture. If you have less, you may become just an employee. Unfortunately, as you have seen earlier in this book, if you have invested hard cash for your minority equity position, you are an economic prisoner, since a minority equity position usually has little or no cash value in the average small start-up. You will likely have no say in running the business and may have no place to sell your stock. This is obviously not quite as true if you are a bit player in a rocket shot like an Intel or a Microsoft. There are always exceptions to every rule. Sometimes, simple luck makes the difference.

If you must use OPM (Other People's Money) to start your business venture, and if you are successful and clever enough, you may be able to maintain control of your company with less than 50% ownership. But even if you don't, you may win a big enough financial stake to move on to a venture that you can control. The "bootstrap" approach worked for me! My win at Varo, though not large, gave me the financial ammo I needed to go forward with my own business.

You must recognize the necessity of having some capital of your own before you try to get started. Other People's Money may generate an Other People's Business. You want what you start to belong to you: So, start saving today so you can go start something in the future!

CHAPTER 7

LUCK

Luck and chance are huge factors in our lives and especially in our business decisions. All the planning that gets done can be nullified by a stroke of bad luck. So, luck must be considered as a partner in anything you do.

A banker friend once told me that it was far better to be lucky than smart!

Almost everything we encounter in life is inevitably influenced by probability and chance, frequently called luck. Regrettably, luck can be both good and bad. Luck is one of those critical chance items that can dramatically change your life. It pops up even when you are not out looking for it. You may or may not recognize it. There is another great word that I have always liked, serendipity. Serendipity means that you find something other than what you were looking for, but as a result of your actually being out looking for something. Serendipitous findings sometimes are the very best opportunities. You need to be aware that luck, chance and serendipity are major factors in everything you do in your success . . . or failure.

The role of luck and chance in our lives is not always recognized for the importance that it has. A number of years ago, perhaps as many as 40 years ago, a graduate student at a major university did research on the question of luck. Luck seems like an odd subject for research to complete a master's or doctoral thesis. However, there were some very interesting findings that came from this work. The researcher determined that the role of luck in successful people's lives is highly underrated and frequently misunderstood. After this researcher developed his study profile and begin to deal with people he discovered some interesting facts. (For more on chance, see *The Drunkard's Walk*, by Leonard Mlodinow; it is available on Amazon.com.)

The first thing the researcher did was to study the profile of those persons who considered themselves lucky and those who consider themselves unlucky, the two extremes. He obviously wanted to draw the maximum contrast between the two for purposes of making his argument. Interestingly, once he did the profiling and completed the study, the one criterion that seemed to dominate a person's perception of their own luck was the number of acquaintances he/she had. People who considered themselves lucky had a large number of acquaintances; and people who considered themselves unlucky tended to be loners. This is a very important concept and one that can change your life. There were a variety of other findings that I have forgotten, but this one item I think is very significant.

In order to place yourself in the lucky mode, you need to develop a broad range of acquaintances. There are many ways to increase the number of acquaintances that you have. Many people develop the skill of making friends naturally. If, on the other hand, you need coaching in how to develop acquaintances, you can consider the possibility of joining a church, service club or any other form of organized activity. Volunteer work can bring you into contact with a lot of people with different points of view. There are huge numbers of volunteer opportunities in today's society. Hobby organizations are another pleasant way to meet many people who share like interests.

The reason why the number of acquaintances is so important is that the more people you know, the more new ideas and serendipitous opportunities you will be exposed to. Opportunities may be brought to you by a friend who sees things that you may or may not have seen. The friend exposing the opportunity may not even see his idea as an opportunity for himself since he lacks your unique point of view. A large number of acquaintances means that lots of eyes and brains out there are unknowingly working on your behalf. They might come upon ideas and advice for you on purpose, or more likely, just accidentally. Further, once an idea comes along that you think you might wish to follow up on, having a large number of acquaintances means that you have a lot of people to check out the idea with and get opinions. Sometimes your friends will bring your feet back to the ground on an idea that you think is spectacular but might really be a bad idea to begin with. I will discuss mentoring later, but a good mentor can be very helpful in sorting ideas.

So, I urge you throughout your career to seek ways to expand the number of people that you know. Keep a phone book on your desk or a contact list on your computer and keep everybody you meet in it. Always ask for a business card and give one. If you use the computer for your records, log everybody into your contacts. Keep notes in the same file that reflect some important thing about that person, so that when you do call him/her, you have some odd fact about him. That makes him think that you remember him very personally and very clearly. You may only remember one piece of contact data but, if necessary, you can easily search out the contact in your computerized file for additional information.

There are many available card readers and programs that make logging of business cards a snap. Another good rule is to generate a variety of email distribution lists so that you can contact numerous people with specific items of interest to either you or them. Email is a great tool if it's not abused.

People like to be recognized and remembered, and they never tire of hearing their name or your comments about their accomplishments. So, if you can call them by name and mention some accomplishment that you can recall, you will be way, way ahead of the game. Computer contact files are golden. The best recognition you can give to a person is recalling their name. In my opinion, being able to remember a person's name is the ultimate form of recognition. They will notice!

Good ideas and good opportunities generally do not come with labels or flashing neon signs. Just the slightest hint may come into your peripheral vision as a result of things you read or people you visit with. Spotting a business opportunity out of these noisy sources is an interesting experiment in the role of chance, luck and serendipity in our lives.

While I strongly suggest that you make every personal effort to join as many different organizations and develop as many friendships and acquaintances as possible, you must be careful not to dissipate energy on useless activity. Some organizations, hobbies and volunteer jobs can absorb tremendous amounts of your time with little benefit. It's a delicate balance, but in my view, the balance leans heavily toward having a wide variety of acquaintances.

One of the biggest problems for entrepreneurs is that most ideas are bad ideas. Some are very bad ideas. Sorting the flow of ideas and opportunities into ones that are truly workable is an art. Most entrepreneurs who fail in a start-up go under because of lack of adequate cash or because bad business choices were made initially, resulting from a combination of bad judgment, weak ideas or just plain bad luck. Luck is always at work in our lives! We get the best results when we take advantage of our good luck.

Unfortunately, a new business idea can look good great at the outset, but it may turn out to be a really bad idea. So, careful reviews of business plans and deep discussions with trusted business friends and mentors are very important to help sort out those ideas that do have real promise and help you avoid the bad idea traps. Still, your intuition is a formidable weapon in finding the right place to start. All the analysis in the world cannot replace your intuition and your careful judgment based on a healthy mix of intuition and facts. Luck also has its limits so pay attention to the details.

If you study your own life, you will find that many of the most important events in your life came about as a result of some minor unplanned happening. For example, I met my future wife on a blind date; we have been married more than 55 years. In fact, I have met quite a number of other people who met their spouses the same way. That is clearly serendipity. Business opportunities can happen the same way. A casual comment by a friend might be enough to spark an idea that could lead to a powerful business opportunity or business connection.

I know that business schools focus on rigorous, detailed planning and careful execution, and there's nothing wrong with that approach. Still, the truly rare opportunities seem to come almost out of nowhere. Great ideas just pop into people's heads. That is why the development of many acquaintances is such a powerful tool for the entrepreneur; ideas flow from all directions. Do not let your plans be so fixed that you overlook what might be an incredible opportunity.

In my personal experience, my job at Texas Instruments came from a casual comment by a distant friend. My move to Varo two and one-half years later came about from an over-the-back-alley-fence conversation between one of my Texas Instruments friends and his neighbor. The neighbor had heard that a company in Garland, Texas, Varo Inc., was looking for someone to design and manufacture specialized semiconductor devices for military night-vision equipment (the Starlight Scope). That was a very tenuous connection but it really paid off for me.

My contact with Fuji Electric 17 years later came about as the result of a sales call to Toshiba in Japan. On a factory visit in Japan, I had noted that Toshiba had a competing product on the production line. When I asked about the source, I was informed that the products were from Fuji Electric. Shortly thereafter, when I left Varo, I immediately made contact with the Fuji office in Tokyo with the thought of importing their products for the North American market. That resulted in an incredibly good 25-year relationship. All of this resulted from a long string of accidental, serendipitous and lucky contacts. Opportunity, serendipity and luck have been companions throughout my life. I am a thoughtful planner and goal setter, but I recognize the finite nature of my preconceived plans. As my banker friend once said, "Lucky is better than smart."

Well, I think you need to be a little bit of both. Usually, in my opinion, luck favors those who are well-prepared and have lots of acquaintances and business contacts.

You cannot build a business depending on luck, but you must be aware that luck is always working either for you or against you. Good planning can annul the effect of bad luck but might not be able to stop it. Allow room in your plans for opportunity and pray for good luck!

CHAPTER 8

MENTORS

You choose your mentors; do not let them choose you! There are few things in your business career that will serve you better than good mentors. Good mentors can be the difference between success and failure as you start a business. Seek the very best advice you can find.

Seeking mentors is a critical step in your business and personal life. Good advice can be critical for any new venture. You may have only yourself as the sole employee in the new business for a while as you get underway. If you are a one-man operation, you cannot rely on your employees for their judgment. If you have a few employees, they may be inexperienced and they are too likely to try to tell you what they think you want to hear. A mentor can criticize your ideas without any fear of reprisal.

There are a number of organizations set up to provide access to potential mentoring. Young Presidents Organization (YPO) is one of the best. There are many organized executive and CEO councils in larger cities. Members of these groups seek to expand the educational, mentoring and idea exchange opportunities among their members. I had the opportunity to participate in YPO for many years and it was one of the best experiences of my life.

In fact, though I have been out of YPO for over 25 years, I still maintain YPO contacts through a Senior YPO/WPO forum. Our forum has been together for more than 30 years. We have had a few new members added and a few lost, but the bulk of us still meet on a monthly basis to discuss various issues, mostly personal now since most of us are retired. Back in our heyday, the forum discussions were all business. But being part of this group today is still very important to me and I look forward to every meeting. You need to have some activity in your life that takes on this level of importance. A group of this type can function as your unofficial board of directors.

If you do not belong to any service organizations as of now, one of the best ones to consider is your local Rotary Club. Rotary Clubs began 100 years ago for the purpose of linking business people for the express purpose of networking and opening new business opportunities. Rotary Clubs also have a very good volunteer program for service work. You will undoubtedly find a Rotary Club very near your home or office. If you are interested in expanding your speaking abilities along with expanding your business contacts, consider a Toastmasters Club membership. There may be as many Toastmasters Clubs as Rotary Clubs, so finding one in your immediate vicinity should be an easy task using one of the available search engines on the Internet.

Today there are many other social and business opportunities that can be easily accessed through electronic-media. Still, I think face-to-face contact is far superior and membership in a service club is an idea that will work for you. In almost every community there are multiple opportunities for volunteer involvement. Any of these volunteer jobs will help generate contacts that may be helpful in your early business life. There is also the possibility of developing lifelong friendships.

Organized activity is not the only way to access mentors. My rule has always been that if I spotted an individual whom I would like to have as one of my mentors, whether I knew him or not, I would approach him with a request for "advice" on a specific issue. Very few people can resist a plea for advice. That is a good first step in acquiring a mentor. If you find a mutual rapport, you can seek future advice from this individual and you will have successfully recruited a new mentor. It is that easy! Remember, acquiring a mentor is your personal responsibility, not the mentor's responsibility. You may need a mentor for helping on just one issue or perhaps you want to develop a continuing relationship. Either way, there is no substitute for aggressive recruitment. Ask for advice and you will almost always get it! Most people are flattered by a request for advice.

A really powerful mentoring relationship can graduate into friendship and, if you are really lucky, "sponsorship." The difference between a mentor and a sponsor is more than one of degree. A sponsor begins to take responsibility for your future, actively advising and directing your thinking and helping you seek new opportunities. I have had many mentors of my choosing, but I couldn't choose a sponsor, the sponsors had to choose me.

I was working as a volunteer on a capital fundraising drive at the Dallas Jesuit high school back in 1983. We had seven o'clock Monday morning meetings every week to report and put pressure on all of us to get the job done. One of the other members of that group was a gentleman named Bill Cooper. I had met Bill previously and had a nodding relationship with him but had not gotten to know him well. We were the early birds at the Monday morning meetings, and as we got to know each other better, we discovered that we were both pilots. There is a special relationship between pilots. Bill had flown B-29s in World War II and was still flying privately. I was also flying privately and doing a few airshows at that time. I approached Bill as a mentor, as he had been extremely successful in his business career and I had many questions for him to help me in my own business career.

After a bit of mentoring, the budding friendship developed into sponsorship. Bill suggested that I join the Dallas Chamber of Commerce aviation committee as its chairman. In fact, the committee did not really exist, but efforts were needed to preserve aviation at Dallas Love Field. Southwest Airlines was under extreme pressure from the Dallas City Council at that time. Under Bill's sponsorship, I became chairman of the aviation committee and spent many hours and days working with the Chamber and the Dallas City Council to preserve Love Field. Three years later I became a member of the Board of Directors of the Chamber and finally its Chairman in 1988. Along the way, I became a director of Dallas-Fort Worth International Airport. So the person that I picked as a mentor eventually became a sponsor and changed the entire trajectory of my life. That's the power of picking your own mentors.

While you can sometimes choose your mentor, you cannot choose a sponsor; he has to pick you. I was lucky enough to acquire a small number of sponsors, especially Bill Cooper, all of whom guided and pushed me into many areas of opportunity. Bill was more like a father to me than a mentor or sponsor. He was a strong father figure in my life but without all the family baggage to deal with! He was free with his advice and criticism. I needed that.

Young entrepreneurs, whether they realize it or not, desperately need an array of mentors to deal with all the complexities that are inevitable in a fledgling business. The amazing thing is that so many people welcome the opportunity to give advice to a willing listener. One great advantage of using mentors is that they have no hourly billing rate, unlike your lawyers or accountants who turn on the rate meter with every phone call. A good mentor can also be a friend for life and, if you're very lucky, develop into a sponsor.

Honesty is critical for all phases of business life, but is most critical to a good mentoring relationship. Anyone interested in helping you solve your problems will have a very sensitive BS detector. Never give a mentor any cause to doubt your honesty. This is good advice for all aspects of your business and personal life. Benjamin Franklin said "Honesty is the best policy." It is! Nothing can destroy your business future as quickly as just one dishonest act. That doesn't rule out being tactful in a relationship, but the truth should never be hidden. Tactfulness is the art of telling the truth without being blunt or hurtful. Tact is one of those behaviors that a good entrepreneur needs to master.

Your time and energy will be rewarded when you seek mentors. Mentors, and perhaps sponsors, can change your life and change your probabilities of success dramatically. Plus, you may develop some really lasting friendships in the process. That is a real bonus!

CHAPTER 9

THE LAW OF UNINTENDED CONSEQUENCES

Almost every action in any business has more than one consequence. A critical awareness of the potential unintended consequences before action is taken can be a lifesaver. Unexpected things always happen, but with careful prior attention, many resulting problems can be avoided.

You cannot change just one thing, no matter how hard you try. There will almost always be some consequence that you did not anticipate at the time a decision was made or action taken. That means you must be alert to the unexpected consequences of everything you do. It's an immutable rule. It has many manifestations but the most critical one is that it behaves like a landmine; you accidentally step on it and it blows up. There is no way to completely avoid unexpected consequences, but if you are alert to the possibilities, you have a better chance of correction before significant damage is done.

One of the more interesting ways that unintended consequences work their way into your life is "malicious obedience." If your instructions to a subordinate are too specific, the subordinate might very well carry your orders out exactly as given, even though he sees a nasty unintended consequence coming. He may go ahead just to prove that you are an idiot for giving him such detailed instructions and not relying on a bit of judgment on his part. So, you must always let your employees know you expect them to use good judgment. If an individual cannot understand what you mean by good judgment, you have probably hired the wrong person.

There is an apocryphal story of a truck driver that illustrates how destructive malicious obedience can be. His boss gave him very specific instructions on how to get to a particular destination for a delivery. En route, he came across a road construction project blocking his path. The boss had told him to go to his destination by a very specific route and he did exactly that, driving through the unexpected construction area and breaking the truck's axle, a very expensive mistake. His answer was: "Boss, that's the way you told me to go, so I did." Malicious obedience! He succeeded in making the boss look bad, but in that particular case, he was fired, so he didn't get quite the result from his actions that he intended. He lost his job. That's exactly what should happen to anyone who commits malicious obedience. The firing doesn't erase the boss's responsibility to have given clear advice to his people to use common sense at all times.

Many years ago, I heard that Nordstrom's department store in San Francisco had a policy manual that consisted of one page and one paragraph. That one policy item stated that every employee would be held responsible for using their good judgment at all times. That is really the only policy that a small business needs. Of course, there are government rules and regulations that have to be followed, but as far as behavioral policy goes, the requirement of always using good judgment is foremost.

On the other hand, there is a lot to be said for following established practices and procedures. Most of the time your employees' good judgment should ensure that they do exactly that. Most practices and procedures, especially in manufacturing, are the result of broad testing and experimentation before implementation.

This is particularly true in all technical laboratory and chemical processes.

My early experiences in manufacturing showed me how easy it is to generate unintended consequences. We dealt with very complex chemical and physical processes to manufacture semiconductor devices. There might easily be several hundred steps in any given process. An unwary engineer might decide to make one small change in one step and not realize that every step thereafter would be affected. That lack of judgment could, and sometimes did, shut down the production line until the unwise change could be found and corrected. We tried to stress to all of our people that you cannot change *just one thing*. If you change one thing, there are always other things that will change, too, even though you did not intend it.

One example of this potentially devastating effect centered around the use of a silicone varnish on one of our semiconductor devices. We determined that in order to get the desired outcome the oven curing temperature of the varnish had to be 200°C. One of our engineers had come from another company and he knew that the varnish curing specification published by the manufacturer, General Electric, recommended a maximum curing temperature of 150°C.

That engineer kept trying to change the process, but wary manufacturing personnel would always report him to his boss or to me, and he would be stopped before the process change was implemented. When I left the company in 1978, one of the first things this gentleman did was to go back to the ovens and turn the temperature down to 150°C. Before it was determined what had happened, almost 90 days of production of that particular product was lost. It's the little things that count in process work and you truly can't change *just one thing*. But the idea applies to far more than manufacturing processes. His judgment was faulty for not following well-established procedures.

In any company, there will be many small opportunities for malicious obedience to raise its ugly head. Similarly, the law of unintended consequences will manifest itself over and over. Sensitivity to these two problems might help avoid some of the pitfalls. The insistence on individual use of good judgment is still a good antidote to unintended consequences in most cases.

Maintain a careful awareness of the possibility of unintended consequences as you make business decisions. You will never avoid this problem 100%, but you can certainly improve your rate of success in avoiding many of the pitfalls through constant vigilance and the absolute awareness that you cannot change just one thing!

DELEGATION

Getting any job done takes a significant amount of effort and may involve a number of people; therefore, delegation of authority and responsibility is frequently a necessity. Delegation is the technique used to get a coordinated effort from a large number of people. Delegation is an art as much as it is a science. Time spent getting it right will be rewarded. Delegation is absolutely essential to effective and efficient operations.

Even experienced managers frequently do not understand the process of delegation. Delegation is the art of avoiding being the "doer" but becoming a "have-doner." Unless you can become reasonably competent in the art of delegation, you will not be able to develop a significant business. One person can only do so much. Eventually, in a successful business, you will have employees who can carry out the various missions of the business based on your plan. Delegation implies making assignments, and even more critically, following up. Follow-up is absolutely essential for successful delegation. Failure to follow up well severely limits your ability as a manager.

Almost 40 years ago, two gentlemen, William Oncken, Jr., and Don Wass, published an article in the *Harvard Business Review* then titled: "The Care and Feeding of Monkeys." This article is one of the most reproduced articles from the *HBR*. It is still available on the Internet. (See Amazon.com title: *Management Time: Who's Got the Monkey?*) I highly recommend acquiring this article and giving it your careful study. At one time, Don Wass gave seminars on delegation utilizing the monkey concept popularized in this article. Don was a gifted showman and his presentation was stunning. I had all my managers attend a full one-day seminar with him. Their approach to delegation was greatly improved with exposure to these concepts.

The basic idea in the article is that a job to be delegated is a monkey on your back. Your objective is to pass the monkey to a subordinate and have the monkey stay with the subordinate. The subordinate's reporting of progress on the delegated project for your evaluation is how you feed and care for the monkey. If you offer to do some parts of the work, or even if you just offer to think about it, the monkey may jump back onto your shoulders. The object of delegation is to be absolutely certain in every boss/subordinate transaction that the monkey stays where it belongs: on the subordinate's shoulders. You will be amazed at the imagery that you get from reading this article. I strongly urge that you read it, believe it and practice it. Delegation is a learned art and is not instinctive. You probably didn't learn it in engineering or business school either. You must develop it on your own.

At the beginning of a relatively small entrepreneurial venture, there may be so few employees that you may not think delegation is much of an issue. Still, from the day you hire your first employee, your skill at delegation will be a major factor in the future success of your business. Even though you try to share your vision for the company, most employees will never have a complete grasp of it. Your ability to delegate will determine whether they are successfully able to understand what their job is and what you expect. Your systematic follow-up, the care and feeding of the monkey, will give them the courage to continue forward. Subordinates expect and learn from good follow-up. They also expect you to give a clearly defined vision to them. If you think you do not have time to delegate or followup, you are wrong. It is one of the very best uses of your time. For you and your subordinates, the caveat applies: If you don't know where you're going, any road will do. Thus, the effort expended to be clear in your delegation will help focus both you and the employees' efforts into a productive vein.

I have heard comments many times from employees that their direct boss failed to properly delegate work to them and followup in a timely manner. This left them unclear as to what was expected. It is essential that you learn the delegation process well. Clear communication to your subordinates is absolutely essential to success. Remember, it's your cash that is at stake and you are the one who is responsible for the success of the enterprise.

Early in my manufacturing career, I had a factory supervisor who did not believe in setting clear work goals and production standards for his factory workers. I insisted that standards be developed for each and every task and output be measured against time. He resisted, but followed through and got it done. Amazingly, he came to me later and told me that he was certainly glad that the standard-setting had been forced on him, since his employees remarked that now they knew what was expected of them. This is a low-grade form of delegation but it is very important. People want to know what you expect of them. Delegation and follow-up are the way to get expectations and performance clearly aligned.

Many years ago I was invited to our local bank for a seminar conducted by a business school professor from Texas A&M University. He dealt with a lot of issues, but the one idea that I found extremely valuable was the concept of charting progress on any performance criterion that you consider to be particularly important for an employee or employee group.

The professor urged that the boss have the individual responsible for a critical task develop his own progress chart for the intended item of focus and post it in the vicinity of his desk. His job was to keep the chart up to date. My job was to look at that chart at least once a week and perhaps make some comment. But just looking was good enough, according to the professor.

I tried it and it worked like magic.

At the time, our company was relatively small and our lone accountant was responsible for all the financial processes of the business, including customer collections. Accounts receivable were then sitting out at a bit beyond 60 days under his guidance. He really did not like to call people and ask them to pay their bills. Unfortunately, calling is an absolute requirement, since many customers will not pay until after they have had a call or two. I know that is regrettable, but it is simply true.

Once he developed the chart of aged receivables and posted it over his desk, and I had a chance to look and comment a few times, our receivables came down to the 30-day level within just a few weeks. I've used that same idea many times to get specific performance from individuals who have some critical task that they are deficient in. A posted and maintained chart of progress truly motivates employees without being punitive. The best part of this technique is that it takes almost no conversation to get the job done; you only have to look at the chart weekly and act interested. Most people enjoy taking pride in their personal progress. Charting allows you to take advantage of that feeling. By the way, charting your own progress is a good way to motivate yourself.

Many successful Japanese companies have mastered the art of charting statistical progress in almost every sector of their businesses, from manufacturing and quality control to the accuracy of administrative documents. There are companies every year in Japan that strive to receive a special award, the Deming Prize, named for W. Edwards Deming, the father of statistical quality control. Deming's work was not recognized early in the United States, but was seized upon by the Japanese as a method of improving the quality of their products in the 1960s. The Japanese Deming Prize is awarded to those companies that can show extreme progress in their ability to document and chart virtually every aspect of their business in order to maintain high output and sterling quality control. The Deming process is challenging and requires dedicated effort by both management and workers, but it produces great results.

After World War II, Japanese products coming into the United States were of very low quality. The early Japanese automobiles and stereo equipment simply fell apart after a short time. Deming's efforts in Japan turned the manufacturing quality situation around to the point that Japanese automobile and audio manufacturers became the very best in the world from both a quality and performance point of view. Sony was one of the earliest examples of rapidly improving Japanese quality control. Sony became the absolute master and the benchmark for quality audio and video devices. In the automotive field, Toyota has become one of the best-selling series of vehicles in America, competing with American companies on a very strong basis from low-cost to luxury cars. It seems that you now see more Lexus automobiles on the road than Cadillacs. American auto manufacturers, under extreme competitive pressure, have rapidly caught up with Japanese quality.

There is no doubt that clear delegation, the setting of clear performance and quality expectations, careful charting and detailed follow-up can produce extraordinary results. Even the smallest start-up company can profit from these ideas. It's a well-established fact that American and world markets will not accept sloppy performance or poor quality these days. Excellence is expected, and nothing less will do.

Spend some time studying successful managers and learn their habits of delegation. Study William Oncken's monkey story. Work on the process. It's one area that the average manager can always improve, and it's the one area that is absolutely essential for the successful entrepreneur. **Delegation is one of the most difficult techniques to master for the typical entrepreneur who wants to do everything himself. When you delegate, you must follow up; delegate, don't abdicate. You will quickly find that it's far better to be a great have-doner rather than a great doer!**

INCLUSION AND RECOGNITION

"Chapter 11" may seem like a bad title for a chapter heading in a book on entrepreneurial management and financial issue! Well, maybe not . . . Mastering the concept of inclusion will guarantee you the best chance at success in your decision-making process and the avoidance of the "other" chapter 11. Many inputs are always better than just one or two. Another advantage of inclusion is that your associates will be flattered by your interest in what they have to say and their dedication to the company's interests will grow!

As a result of this being Chapter 11, I hope that you don't think that any of the information contained in this chapter is "bankrupt"! Nevertheless, it is a sad fact that many an entrepreneurial business start-up ends up facing bankruptcy. But I won't deal with that issue in this chapter. In fact, I don't intend to deal with the bankruptcy issue at all. That is a total default situation in the entrepreneurial world. I'm talking about success and how to achieve it. I'll let the lawyers take care of bankruptcy! I will also pray that you can avoid failure, at least most of the time.

Running a business is a very complex process and has to be taken very seriously. There is no perfect formula, but inclusion and recognition of employees is a good start to help avoid many of the pitfalls that lie in front of any new business. A good measure of any manager's capability is the level to which he is inclusive. He must include his people in decision-making and be willing to give them recognition for their advice and their individual successes. Even a very small entrepreneurial company must be careful with these issues. Nothing demoralizes employees more than not being asked for their opinion and then not being recognized for their useful ideas and personal accomplishments.

A failure of inclusion is one of those things that most often results from simple human-relations negligence, a failure to think of the impact of the boss's decisions on subordinates. If the employees know a bit in advance what is being planned, and have a small part in the decision-making process, they might be more willing to accept the decision when it is made. Their opinions are likely to have a positive influence on the direction of the decision and the eventual success of the business.

Good ideas are not the private property of the boss. I am critically aware that meetings can absorb an inordinate amount of time and be relatively pointless. But some meetings are required to satisfy the need to include subordinates in the management process. As a business grows, this issue becomes even more critical. Careful attention needs to be paid to the process of communication and inclusion. The grapevine inside the company is a very important tool for the sensitive manager. It's a good idea to listen to the grapevine and to have an access point on the grapevine for you to occasionally feed back information. There's always somebody willing to do that task.

Formal meetings are not always required to generate a climate of inclusion. Just mentioning an issue on the fly can frequently accomplish the inclusion that is so important. So long as a subordinate gets some chance to act or object before the decision is made, they are more likely to be a good team player and go along with the final decision.

One of the key skills that any manager needs to develop is the art of conducting a meeting. Without good planning, any meeting can be a total waste of time. The person conducting the meeting should have a clear outline of the issues that need work. Even better, the meeting points should be summarized in writing and distributed to the participants. Whiteboards with colored markers are a great asset to enhance communication in meetings. The ability to put key points on the board is especially important if there is a brainstorming component in the meeting. Also consider using various media tools such as *Elluminates* or *Go To Meeting* on the web to avoid travel expenses and to include staff in remote locations. Various media also allow you to record the meeting, which can be replayed via the computer at any time for purposes of review and study.

Regardless, having the points on a common readable surface, whether it is on a board or a computer screen that everyone can see, is central to the conduct of productive and efficient meetings. There should be little time allotted in any serious meeting for small talk. Issues should be discussed in a predetermined order, and resolved if possible. The leader of any meeting should approach it with a very positive mental attitude and an open mind.

Every meeting should generate a very clear list of assignments, do-lists. If no next step is planned during a meeting, the meeting has been a waste of time. Any objective worth chasing requires a next step. The same is true for every meeting. Think: What is the logical next step, or perhaps, next steps!

The biggest benefit of a meeting is that meetings generate automatic inclusion. Of course, the right people have to be invited in order to make inclusion work. Leaving out a key person is almost worse than no inclusion effort at all. The excluded individual will probably sulk and be less productive for some period of time. Worst of all, you may never be aware of it.

Inclusion, besides being a great management and problem-solving tool, is the greatest form of recognition in a business environment. Few things enhance individual performance more than recognition from the boss or the owner. The first and most important form of recognition is calling people by their first name. Any manager should be very careful to learn the names of as many of his employees as possible. This is really a very important issue. This could be an easy step early in a business's history since there may be very few people involved. But as time goes by, each new person will be highly motivated if the boss can call them by name.

When it comes to employee recognition, I do not think any company in the world has done a better job than Southwest Airlines in Dallas. Herb Kelleher, the CEO for many years, memorized the names of all of his employees as they were hired. The company now has tens of thousands of employees and I'm not sure Herb has kept up with all the new names. But he has the gift of a flawless memory, and he not only remembers names but key details about each individual. It was like a breath of fresh air to walk through the offices and shops of Southwest Airlines and see Herb greet his employees by their first name.

While most of us do not have that incredible facility (I certainly do not), we need to work at it as our company grows. Any company will be no better than its employees. Recognition programs exert a very large influence in creating and maintaining great employee morale.

Another factor that is important to good morale is company performance. Performance is always the responsibility of the entrepreneur or the CEO. Poor performance will almost always generate low morale; great performance will usually generate great morale. It is very difficult to have high morale and low performance simultaneously. I have rarely seen morale lead the way to superior performance. It's almost always the other way around. Performance leads and morale follows! It's the job of the owner and the key management to get performance rolling. Morale will just about take care of itself at that point.

Another interesting program that Southwest Airlines developed, and that any business should consider mimicking, is an annual recognition banquet. After having attended a couple of these at Southwest, I would not hesitate in recommending to any business student or entrepreneur, before he launched his entrepreneurial effort, that he try to attend a Southwest Airlines recognition banquet. Simple recognition, a certificate, a photograph of Kelleher presenting a service pin to an employee, has had incredible benefits, far more than the cost of the tokens and the banquet.

Give credit to your employees where credit is due and give it amply. It is critical that the boss not claim all the credit to himself. He cannot do it alone and he needs to spread the credit around. The best tool in his bag for company performance is inclusion and individual recognition of good performance.

Another interesting aspect of superior recognition practice is timely termination of seriously underperforming employees. The termination of an employee who is performing poorly will have a profound effect on those employees who remain. His or her fellow employees likely saw the problem long before the boss did and wondered how long it was going to take for the boss to figure it out and terminate the offending individual. The overall morale of the team is almost always improved by a well-deserved firing. This is a strong point to keep in mind as you move forward.

Usually, by the time the boss figures out that it is time to terminate a malefactor, it's already six months beyond a reasonable delay time. All of the terminated employee's associates will feel great satisfaction even though they may not articulate that satisfaction. It's not *schadenfreude;* it's just that no employee likes to see another employee getting away with a poor work ethic. The boss almost always has a strong reluctance to fire anyone. But recognizing the justice and the positive effects of a firing might make a difficult task a bit easier.

By the way, the unpleasant but absolute requirement to terminate poor performers is one good reason not to hire family members or close friends as employees. Firing a family member can cause a tremendous disruption within the family. My recommendation is to only hire strangers, no family and no close friends. Obviously, there are risks in dealing with people you don't know, but if you are very careful in checking out every last detail of the future employee's employment and education history, you can minimize the problem.

Careful fact-checking can pay huge dividends. I remember one situation when we were hiring an administrative individual to work with financial data and marketing in our company. She had a great resume that included a degree from the University of Georgia. When our VP asked for a copy of the individual's college records, she gave us a telephone number for the registrar's office at the University of Georgia. Our VP called and a very friendly voice answered, identifying herself as the university registrar. After some discussion with this individual, our VP's sixth sense cut in and he began to probe more deeply. After a few minutes, the lady on the other end of the phone broke down and admitted that she was our new employee's sister and had reluctantly agreed to play the role of the registrar in the event that we followed up. Neither person had ever had any relationship with the University of Georgia, so careful checking of backgrounds is essential. You can be sure that that individual was no longer with us at the end of the day.

Follow up all references and check with prior employers. While most companies will not give out information regarding performance evaluations of former employees, they will at least confirm or deny the period of employment and possibly tell whether the individual is eligible for rehire. There are many fabricated resumes out there in the personnel marketplace. Don't become a victim of resume fraud. An individual committing resume fraud will very likely do damage to your company and perhaps, in the worst case, embezzle company funds or materials.

If the job in question is very sensitive, it might be a good idea to hire an investigator who does background checking as a profession. There are many sources for this type of help. Most of these organizations can do a really good job and you don't need to involve any of your employees or yourself in the background research process. There is absolutely nothing improper about very careful investigation of future employees. In fact, it is a serious mistake *not* to investigate anyone who would have a sensitive position in your company.

In one case, we terminated a sales manager for fabricating his trip reports. Instead of being out on customer trips, he was in a motel in San Antonio with a girlfriend. He would call a customer with whom he had made appointments to visit, discuss issues with them, and then write up a trip report as if he had been actually present at the customer location.

We discovered the problem when we called one of his customers trying to make contact with him (this was well before cell phones). They said they had not seen him and that he had canceled his visit. When his expense report came in showing that he had made the visit, the alarm bells began ringing. Further investigation turned up all the ugly facts. Once again, he was not with us at the end of that day. We did not bring criminal charges, but we certainly could have. Unfortunately, you will find that district attorneys are not particularly interested in white-collar crime unless it is a really big theft.

Amazingly, this crook got a sales manager's job with another high-tech company in the area. They did not even call us for reference. But even if they had called, we would've simply confirmed dates of his employment to avoid the risk of a lawsuit. The employment laws are perverted in this area, so you need to carefully learn the legal restraints from a good labor attorney to avoid the pitfalls.

Over the years I have had several employees who embezzled from the company. I am always extremely surprised and very disappointed when a story comes out. There is no way to predict that someone will take advantage of their trusted position in your company. Nothing can be 100% certain when it comes to employment issues and money. However, careful reviews of all the data on an employee's application, investigation of all prior employment and references, and gentle questioning in areas where you can do so legally, can help you avoid real problems.

Knowing your employees in depth and seeking their opinions is critical to your entrepreneurial success. You can't do it all yourself, and there a lot of good ideas floating around even in a small company. So, be inclusive in your decision-making and be careful in your hiring practices.

DECISION-MAKING

Make a decision and stick with it. Not!

The core activity for any business manager or entrepreneur is the ability to make good decisions. Decisions are required on a day-in and day-out basis. Bad decisions must be rectified as quickly as possible. Never stick with a bad decision based on principle. Make your decisions based on fact whenever possible, but do not be afraid to rely on your intuition in a crunch.

Any business person, especially the new entrepreneur, will be faced with a myriad of decisions to be made. Decision-making is one of the very fundamental aspects of management, including entrepreneurial management. Decisions must be made regarding finances, marketing, personnel and every other significant area of the business enterprise. Decision-making is not magic. Good decisions generally involve an intelligent person who has assembled as many of the relevant facts as possible, then made a careful study of those facts, evaluated the alternatives and then finally made a decision. The decision process might take a few seconds to a few days or even longer depending on the urgency and complexity of the issues involved. Decision-making may or may not be the holy grail of management but it comes close.

Whether we realize it or not, we make hundreds of micro-decisions every day in our personal lives. The big difference in the business environment is that the decisions become exceedingly more complex and may have many far-reaching personal and financial consequences.

I have heard many people say, make a decision and stick with it. **That is very bad advice!** You certainly do want to stick with a good decision, but if you recognize at some future point that a decision was poorly made, or the facts have changed, you may very well want to reverse course. Recognizing when a decision has gone bad, and making a needed correction, is critical to your success and perhaps even to your survival. Bullheadedness is not the sign of a good decision-maker. When you're wrong, you're wrong. Back up and change your mind. With a careful approach to decision-making you can hope that more than half of your decisions are the right moves. But when you're obviously wrong, admit it, and make the appropriate changes.

Only a fool sticks with a bad decision!

Clearly, it is important to get as many of the relevant facts as possible before making a decision. On the other hand, you do not want to suffer "paralysis from analysis." At some point, even though the facts may be incomplete, time may be critical and you may be forced to make a decision before you think you are really ready. In fact, I think most decisions are made with less than a majority of the facts in hand. You shouldn't be discouraged by this; if your intuition is reasonably good, you will probably produce satisfactory results even with a deficiency of facts. Still, seeking information prior to decision-making is a smart move if time allows. In some cases, a decision must be made immediately. That is just the way business works in real life.

Intuition is an often under-respected aspect of decision-making. Intuition is the sum total of your knowledge and your experience that resides unconsciously, deep inside your brain. Every future decision you make is conditioned by all of your prior knowledge and experience whether you realize it or not. Your subconscious brain is an incredible computer. You can sometimes produce surprisingly good decisions from this deep-seated background information lying hidden in your subconscious.

We call it intuition. But it is really a lot more than that. In fact, as an entrepreneur you will probably be relying more on your intuition than you'd like, since you might not have time to gather many of the facts needed prior to a decision. So, do not be intimidated by being forced to rely on your intuition in a time-critical situation. Women have long been credited as having better intuition than men and this might well be true. However, your intuition, whether male or female, represents a vast reserve of computing power that you may be just barely aware of. Do not forget it's there.

I have mentioned the role of serendipity and the importance of opportunity and luck in decision-making earlier in this book. But I want to say a bit more about these subjects and their effect on decision-making. Every decision gets modified over time through the course of future events. No decision should be so firm that it disallows future opportunity when something good or bad pops up that wasn't in the original plan. I have heard people say, when it comes to luck, the harder I work the luckier I get. That is absolutely true! Opportunity works the same way: It jumps up when you least expect it, and if you keep your mind open, you may spot a new unexpected opportunity in time to take advantage of it.

It's a wonderful combination: opportunity, intuition, serendipity, and just plain luck. You will probably note after a period of time that a lot of your success or failure is tied to these fragile non-rational inputs that are seemingly insignificant at the time but are critical in your decision-making. In an entrepreneurial business you must take advantage of every good opportunity that pops up and avoid the potholes if you can. I also hope that you are totally right in your decision-making every time. I know that is unlikely but that is certainly the goal. Solid rational and sometimes intuition-informed decision-making should be good enough to guarantee your success without an overly large dependence on raw luck. Still, leave room in your thinking for these easy-to-miss non-rational inputs. Great ideas rarely tap you on the shoulder. Be sensitive to your environment and expect to see unplanned opportunities.

One of the profound comments of the 20th century was credited to Yogi Berra: "It is very difficult to do forecasting, especially when it involves the future." Most decision-making requires some notion of the future, a forecast. Forecasts can come from out of the blue or they can come from solid data. Sometimes it's hard to tell the difference. I hope that you will not become so enchanted with forecasts that they are the sole basis on which you make your future plans and decisions.

During the midterm of my career at Varo, upper-level management brought in a new management consulting firm that demanded unusually detailed forecasts and budgets from my division. Our semiconductor business at that time was growing rapidly and its sales and capital spending were totally uncertain. We were operating in the opportunistic mode within a company that thought fixed budgets were a good idea, and their hired consultants were pushing all of the divisions of the company hard in that direction. We knew that any budget that we did in Semiconductor would be obsolete the day after it was printed. The electronics market was changing rapidly and we were leading the way in a line of new power products. Unbelievably, that was not an acceptable answer at corporate headquarters. They demanded a fixed planning document!

My solution to these perceived unrealistic demands was to prepare multiple budgets: the best case, a worst-case, and what we called the most likely. As it turned out, we even beat the best case for a few years. Fortunately, due to my obstinacy and our good results, the consultants left us alone after that, since we were the most profitable division of the company. Frankly, I asked them to get out of my office and stay out! Thankfully, they did just that. At the time, I considered that one of my primary tasks was to keep the consultants out of my division. We knew what we were doing and we knew they did not have a clue. I do not necessarily recommend this approach for middle-management personnel, which I was at that time, but sometimes, when you are sure you are right and can see things that others do not see, you just have to be a little bit bullheaded!

In the business environment you will receive suggestions from many different directions both inside and outside your company. Try to keep your mind open to input. Always consider input, but in the end, as the boss, the final decisions will be yours. Do not be intimidated by people who think they know more than you do. Sometimes they do, and sometimes they do not. But, paraphrasing Harry Truman: The buck stops with you!

CASH FLOW

At the core of your business you will find that one of the most important management decisions you will make is controlling cash flow. Business circumstances always put pressure on your ability to maintain adequate cash on your balance sheet. But cash starvation can mean instant death for the entrepreneur.

The best advice I can give you in running a start-up company is that before you spend even a dollar, take a look into your figurative cigar box. The question is: "Are there available funds there?" If there is money in the box, maybe you can spend a little of it. If there is no money in the box, sorry, you can't spend! Wow, you say, this is a very primitive way to look at cash flow. The business-school boys might scoff at you. Do not pay any attention to them. The last thing you want to do in start-up cash decisions is to rely completely on an inexperienced business-school graduate. He might know the theory very well, but he might just serve to overly complicate your practical problems.

On the other hand, a talented MBA may do an excellent job in helping you analyze your cash flow. But still, I think you would do well to regard the iconography of the cigar box as a very important piece of symbology. You can't spend money if you don't have it. Well, that's not exactly true; with leverage, you can, but you really don't want to incur too much debt early in a new business, if you can avoid it.

Most of us have grown up in the credit-card era and we spend money without much consideration of whether or not we have any cash today. We charge it and move on, the bill comes in later. But, no matter what, the day for reckoning eventually comes. Unfortunately, bad cash decisions can drive your start-up company into early bankruptcy. Even if it does not result in bankruptcy, bad cash management can be totally destabilizing. So, in my opinion, management of cash is the top priority for the emerging entrepreneur. You must be careful in all your cash decisions. Do not let your precious cash get away from you, it is your lifeblood. Believe me; your first employees will really notice your approach to cash management. Do not expect them to be more careful with your money than you are.

If respect for cash doesn't drive your mental processes, you're in for a gigantic surprise. If you run out of cash, new cash is very expensive, if you can get any at all! If you go out and try to raise new money when you are cash-short, you will be a victim! You will feel like you have been raped when it's all over, if you even survive. So, plan your business around cash availability. Cash is king—actually cash is more than king, cash is the most critical issue in a new company. No cash, no business! While I did not place this rule in the number one spot, it is extremely important; you cannot ignore it without risking great peril. You need to keep that figurative cigar box handy so that you can look into it periodically to see whether you can spend or not. No money in the box, you probably can't spend!

I'm well aware that modern businesses tend to operate on a completely different concept of cash. But if you're an entrepreneur, forget that nonsense. Your new business will run on cash, not some abstract theory. If you do not have cash, you are a dead duck, so you'd better pay very careful attention to your cash position every day. I hate being redundant, but this is really important!

Think about it: How would you react to someone coming to you who is broke, that is, out of cash, and wanting your help? You might be willing to help, but your terms would likely be very harsh. If you run out of cash, that's what you will face—very harsh terms for more money, and possibly a loss of control. You need to plan your initial entry into an entrepreneurial business in such a way that you can guarantee yourself that you will avoid cash strangulation. There is no other option; cash is the single most important asset of a new business. I can't stress this enough, running out of cash is the most frequent problem that destroys businesses before they ever get fully started. The reason for cash failure is usually poor planning. But even solid planning can yield to a problem as things change during the start-up process.

I have seen more fledgling businesses destroyed by lack of adequate cash at a point early in their life than any other single factor. You must almost be a fanatic when it comes to conserving your cash. Surely, I know you have to make risky gambles in any new business, but . . . ***do not run out of cash***! And, never bet the company—unless you are betting on a sure thing.

Acquiring too much inventory is a cash-related problem that tends to infect entrepreneurial enterprises early in their life. Too much "stuff" is a disaster, particularly if it is the wrong stuff! Look on your balance sheet; cash, inventory and accounts receivable are the three big current-asset items in most businesses. That means that all the cautions that apply to cash also apply to inventory and receivables. Inventory becomes an anchor if you cannot move it in a reasonable time. Inventory turnover rate is critical. You need to convert inventory into cash on a predictable basis, in a relatively short cycle. If you do not, you will develop a cash flow problem that could kill your business.

The last thing you want to happen is to find yourself in a situation where your assets are inflated with totally valueless inventory. Do not let that happen to you! Like inadequate cash, excess inventory can be a sudden-death experience. In fact, death by inventory may actually be more common than death by cash shortage; cash shortage and excess inventory are more or less synonymous. It is far too easy to convert cash into inventory. The problem with inventory is that you cannot convert it back into cash without a sale. But on the other hand, if you do not have the product in the warehouse, you may miss a big sale. Product in the warehouse, however, does not guarantee sales. Do not be seduced by the continuing perceived need for inventory which might eventually become excess inventory—dead weight on your balance sheet.

Inventory decisions drive the success or failure of a lot of businesses. The urgent need to make new sales will put pressure on decisions about both inventory and the creditworthiness of the customer. Inventory purchased to support a non-paying customer can be a disaster. Careful credit analysis is essential to the emerging business. There are a variety of sources for credit information, and all of them should be utilized. Knowledge of your customer is somewhat of a buffer against credit problems. Do not hesitate to ask the difficult questions when it comes to creditworthiness. Any sale not paid for is a lot worse than no sale. You must take full responsibility for determining creditworthiness of your potential customers and not rely on your sales department. Salesmen frequently just want to book an order; *you* want to book a *profitable order!* You alone are responsible for profitability.

There are a number of major consulting firms that specialize in cycle-time management, the cycle time being from the time inventory is committed until it is sold and the check has cleared the bank. If your business has a production line, inventory fits in the middle of the cycle: initial order, inventory, work-in-progress inventory, shipment and collection. Controlling the overall cycle time, from initial order to cash in the bank, is an essential element of cash management. I have seen it reported that some of these consultants can reduce cycle time by more than 50% in a typical company. I have never personally worked with one of these consulting companies, but at some point in your business's life it might be worthwhile for you to consider a cycle-time consultant.

I have looked at many businesses over the years. The single most striking feature that I have observed is that, frequently, inventory items shown on the balance sheet as assets, are in fact not assets, but are obsolete or unsaleable items. Maintaining inventory as an asset is an appropriate accounting method if the inventory is in fact saleable within a reasonable period. Serious investigation, however, will usually disclose that half or more of the stated inventory may be almost worthless. Don't be a victim! Be aware of your own inventory cycle-time requirements. Good cycle-time management, i.e., fast turnover, minimizes the chances of accumulating excess inventory.

Excess and obsolete inventory are usually generated by faulty projections of future customer demand. Occasionally, while the projections may have been accurate when made, new market situations may demand delivery schedule stretches or cancellations. Bad inventory investment decisions may turn out to be life-and-death decisions for the entrepreneurial business. A small company cannot afford to go bust due to bad inventory decisions. Yet, it happens over and over.

I have been invited many times to look at a business that was available for acquisition only to find that the company balance sheet was totally bogus. Inventory carried as an asset was sometimes nearly valueless. Do not generate bad inventory by careless decisions; that's easy to say, but it is a very critical issue. Long-term viability in any new business will be largely decided by cash and inventory decisions, except, perhaps, in a service business.

For a manufacturing business, I would also recommend that your customer purchasing terms-and-conditions contracts have a provision at the front end of the deal to cover the method of accounting for and paying for any in-process inventory that is stranded due to an order cancellation by the customer. You will find it almost impossible to make a contract modification after the fact. All important requirements for the transaction must be in the original contract.

Remember, when you purchase inventory betting on the come, you're actually betting the company. There is no question that risky spending decisions may be necessary, but sometimes it is required as a condition of doing business. Nevertheless, you must only make that kind of decision after careful consideration. Do not be panicked by your sales department into making a really bad inventory decision.

I wish I could have back all my bad inventory and equipment decisions. That would be worth a few million dollars to me. Most of my decisions have been good, but I have been mouse-trapped into a number of bad inventory and equipment decisions based on very optimistic sales projections. I guess it happens to everyone. I hope it does not happen to you! Think long, hard and carefully about adding new inventory or equipment. You really do not want to bet your company carelessly. At some point you may have to, but do not do it under duress. Think it through.

Managing the cash flow in an entrepreneurial business is a real challenge. Spending money you do not have can lead to sudden death. Seek advice from trusted associates in your cash flow analysis, but recognize that in the final instance, there is no one but you to guard your cash.

14

CONTROL!

If you don't maintain control, in the long term, it's not your company! Control is the very essence of the entrepreneurial lifestyle. Loss of control is the last thing that should happen to an entrepreneur in his own business creation.

I have mentioned control earlier in this book but I would like to discuss it in more depth, since it is an absolutely critical issue for the entrepreneur. Indeed, it is not even worth the effort to start a business, if you the owner, cannot maintain control of it. My definition of control for a small entrepreneurial business is ownership of more than 51% of the voting stock of the company, preferably closer to 100%.

I realize that ownership of a lesser percentage voting stock can deliver control in a large public company, but I am not talking about a large public company in this book. I am talking about the new start-up entrepreneurial company with a limited number of shareholders and a relatively small capitalization at start-up. This book is not intended to deal with really big, highly organized start-ups.

I am most interested in the fledgling entrepreneur entering into his first venture. In my earlier discussion of 50/50 partnerships, I stressed the need for control. Either own the company, or be an employee. I cannot stress this point enough. If you are forced into a minority position, view it as a short-term effort to raise enough capital to move forward and be able to start your own company at some point in the future, one that you own 51% or more of, hopefully 100%.

I had a friend a few years ago who was the CEO of a significant privately-owned, family company, engaged in owning and operating convenience stores. His company had a large number of locations around the Southwest. The company had been founded many years earlier by his grandfather. The stock had been restricted to family members only. However, he personally owned considerably less than 50%.

He made the judgment to build an outside board of directors composed mostly of his old college friends. That actually seems like a pretty good idea, even to me. Everyone can use the efforts of a good board of directors to help sort issues and find opportunities. Investment money, contacts, ideas and direction can come from a board. Rather than do an advisory board, he chose to organize a board in which all of the members had full voting powers. Since some of the board members were very successful people they probably would have declined a purely advisory board position.

Unfortunately, after a while, he began to develop some differences with several members of the board. The outside directors eventually organized the rest of the family directors and shareholders behind his back and fired him. He was later killed in an accident that might have been suicide. I cannot imagine a worse outcome from the loss of control in a closely held business. In my opinion, he would have been far better off to have sold a significant fraction of his position in the company early in his career and started a new company that he would have owned 100%.

This is not an unusual story. Frequently, younger family members are held captive by older members, and when they fail to dance to the tune of the elders, they are unceremoniously fired. Worse, they may be retained with golden handcuffs and abused on a daily basis by disgruntled family members. I can't imagine living in those kinds of conditions, but I have more than one friend in that trap today and others who have managed to escape the trap. Multiple family partners are almost always a very big problem. The best approach is to sell out as quickly as possible and escape to start your own business with the proceeds.

Generally speaking, many beginning entrepreneurs do not understand the need to maintain control until it is too late. I guess some people fear that they might be regarded as control freaks, excessively control oriented. But, in most businesses, there *must be* one controlling point of view, and hopefully, that is the founder/ CEO's point of view. In a very small company, control will be in the hands of whoever owns more than 51%. This is such an important point. Not everyone will tell you this so forcefully, and some will argue the point. I stand on this opinion and feel strongly that *control is critical* to your long-term success as an entrepreneur.

To be a successful and happy entrepreneur, you must have absolute control. Fight for it. Do not go start something without it. Take an indelible marker and write "control" on the front of this book in large letters. You simply cannot forget control as you try to put a business together. If you fail to have and maintain control, you almost certainly will be held hostage by the other owners at some point, particularly if you're successful. Success frequently degrades into debilitating infighting inside privately held companies where the control is not in the hands of one person who can make clear-cut decisions as to the path to be followed.

Fights within companies, particularly fights within families, are terribly destructive, emotionally and financially, to any business. There is almost no way to keep fights private, and customers and banks may be frightened away when they become aware of these destabilizing situations. You can avoid the fights if your word is law.

That means you can avoid these fights only if you have absolute control.

Do not let anybody tell you differently. Do not worry about being called an autocrat. The people who call you that are the very people who you need to worry about. This may sound a bit harsh, but it is simply reality. Criticism is going on every day and almost certainly you have encountered it if you have been around the business world for a while. Consider, but then ignore most of the criticism. This idea may be the most important of this book. A loss of control can certainly lead you into one the most debilitating emotional and financial situations you will ever experience.

Control, control, control! Exert whatever effort it takes on your part to maintain control of your business. Loss of control is loss of control . . . do not let it happen to you!

CALENDAR FREEDOM AND TIME FOR PLAY

While ownership and control are critically important for the entrepreneur, there is a second kind of issue related to absolute control that is a tremendous fringe benefit. Early on in this book I mentioned the huge benefit for you, the entrepreneur, of being able to set and manage your own schedule and calendar and to set your own priorities. I suggested that calendar control might be the most important fringe benefit of entrepreneurial success, and a good reason to consider the entrepreneurial lifestyle.

Life is far more enjoyable if the only people that you have to jump for are your customers and perhaps your bank or spouse. You will lead a much more pleasant life than that of the harried mid-level manager in a large company who has peers and superiors on all sides screaming at him, jerking his chain and in general giving him grief that he can do nothing about except grind his teeth in frustration. I have known so many people caught in these middle-management situations and they all live in deep frustration. The same negative result will come from having less than full control if your ownership in a business is less than 50%.

Entrepreneurs with complete majority control, on the other hand, can have a great sense of personal freedom and a very enjoyable lifestyle. Of course, the ability to move freely depends on success.

If you consider all my **rules**, my 50-item checklist, before you start, I think you are far more likely to avoid the major pitfalls and to make a success of your entrepreneurial start-up business. The rewards of entrepreneurial effort are so great that I strongly urge you to absorb the rules and *go start something.*

Newspapers and magazines are full of stories about entrepreneurs and their toys. Rarely, if ever, will we read of a corporate executive having such a good time. The public CEO's stockholders would go insane and demand his removal. But, a really smart entrepreneur keeps his success and his excesses out of the newspapers. There is no lasting benefit in setting yourself up as a big target for criticism. There are too many ways to enjoy your success that don't need to end up in the face of the press or the public.

The CEO of a large public company is always in the gunsights of media, investors, customers and employees. That doesn't sound like much fun to me. The corporate CEO has every detail of his status and compensation made public by law. Criticism can be abundant from both stockholders and the news media. Anything perceived as a personal excess by the CEO is immediately criticized in a public company. It takes a really thick skin to endure this type of harassment.

Of course, the Hollywood crowd and their fellow travelers crave notoriety as an end in itself. Some corporate CEOs fall into the same category and there is a track record of some very illustrious entrepreneurs doing the same thing. Unfortunately for the CEOs of publicly held corporations, these excesses may become public shortly before the CEO is removed or just after! A recent CEO of Boeing experienced just this disaster.

I personally think that getting a lot of non-business publicity is a mistake for the average entrepreneur. Conspicuous consumption has never been a great idea. It invites serious criticism. However, a few people outside of Hollywood have made it really work; think

Donald Trump, and Sir Richard Branson of Virgin Airlines. Few people can match the excesses of "the Donald" and get away with it! I doubt that any reader of this book will seriously pursue that kind of a dream. I certainly hope not. Fame is toxic and addictive. Loss of privacy is one of the biggest losses you can experience. Being famous is fun to think about but loses some of its charm when privacy is invaded.

Along with control of one's personal calendar, the opportunity for an entrepreneur to enjoy his leisure is a built-in advantage of the entrepreneurial lifestyle. There are many opportunities for friendships of a lasting nature among other entrepreneurs. The whole entrepreneurial world is a bit like a huge club. There are many organizations that cater to the successful entrepreneur, for example, the Young Presidents Organization and its many clones. Several of my very best friends and advisers acquired over the years came as a result of the executives I met in YPO. Membership in these organizations requires jumping through some business and social hoops, but membership in one of these low-profile organizations is well worth it if you can qualify. There are also a variety of other less pricey organizations that offer self-help, education and entertainment opportunities for the entrepreneur.

The true beauty of being a successful entrepreneur is that you will encounter a whole new range of business and social choices without encountering public criticism and without hitting the front pages of the local newspaper. The entrepreneur has few if any of these problems if he is relatively discreet.

I have observed over the years that generally, the mental health of entrepreneurs is substantially better than any other class of people, whether workers or management. In my opinion, freedom in setting your own calendar, which gives you the ability to fish or play golf or participate in any other form of recreation or family activity without inviting criticism, may be the fundamental reason for the entrepreneur's better mental health and positive mental attitude.

If everything you do is subject to scrutiny by a whole range of interests, having fun gets to be very difficult. I am not suggesting that the entrepreneurial lifestyle should be entered just for the fun of it; there is abundant hard work involved. But clearly success as an entrepreneur will yield a much better lifestyle than almost any other path in life. Most entrepreneurs work extremely hard and tend to play extremely hard throughout their careers. I have rarely encountered a successful entrepreneur who doesn't use the word *fun* to describe what he's doing in his business. Every aspect of life improves for the entrepreneur once you are successful.

As a successful entrepreneur you have the ability to do somewhat as you please. You do not have to ask permission or hide when you take time off. Of course, you must maintain good relationships with your employees. They will respect your hard work and tolerate your play . . . if they find out about it. Never flaunt your success inside your company. You can probably stay out of public sight as a basic condition of your entrepreneurial lifestyle unless you choose to seek publicity. As an executive in a public corporation you are public whether you like it or not. That's just a fact of life.

An entrepreneur can do charitable work and make donations without being bound by corporate policy. Most corporations put stringent limits on their executives to limit financial support for charitable organizations and virtually ban support for any religious organization. The entrepreneur faces no such barriers. If you have a strong interest in doing charitable work, you have a clear path. You can sit down and writes a check, no questions asked! Of course, you must maintain business profitability and personal integrity too. No executive, either corporate or entrepreneurial, can afford to take his eye off the ball when it comes to running the business.

I have always had a strong inclination to work with charitable, industry and civic organizations, but I found it quite difficult to do that kind of work as a corporate person. Once I was successful as an entrepreneur, I was able to put my energy and cash where my wife and I thought it was needed. What a wonderful feeling that is!

I once asked a development officer at a university how he could tolerate going out every day to seek funds for his institution. He said it was actually quite easy. His job was to show an opportunity to an individual or a group, and if they decided to jump at that opportunity, the donor would feel that it was the best decision he ever made. When the day came that the gift was actually made and announced, the donor almost always considered it to be the best day of his entire life. So my university development friend was just giving generous people opportunities to do good things with their money. By the way, his primary targets were entrepreneurs.

I remember visiting with a development officer at Southern Methodist University a number of years ago and discussing donors for their graduate business programs. He said that 90% of the donations to their graduate management program came from entrepreneurs and only 10% from large corporations. That donation profile was an eye-opener to me. I have been a fundraiser for various nonprofit organizations for many years and I've come to realize that there is no better target for my fundraising efforts than the successful entrepreneur and here was proof positive.

By the way, at that time, 90% of SMU's educational efforts in the MBA program were directed at training students to become corporate officers and managers, and only 10% were dedicated to the development of entrepreneurs and entrepreneurial skills. In light of this, the imbalance among donors was simply incredible. On the other hand, teaching entrepreneurism is extremely difficult. SMU had one of the earliest entrepreneurial programs in the country. Seeing the critical role played by the entrepreneur in our society was the biggest reason I had for putting my ideas together in this book. I hope you find some benefit from this effort.

A few years ago, Prof. Joseph Picken, University of Texas at Dallas, School of Management, initiated an entrepreneurial focus within the university's MBA program. Starting the new program required herculean effort on his part, but he prevailed, and the Institute for Innovation and Entrepreneurship is a reality at UTD. It wasn't easy to start a new program in a state funded institution. In fact, Prof. Picken raised the private funds that were necessary for the initial launch of his program. I was very pleased to have been a part of that effort and I served on the Institute board for three years.

Today, less than a decade after his initiative became reality, there are more than 1,000 students enrolled for courses in the Institute for Innovation and Entrepreneurship. The students come from the various other schools at the University including, of course, the Graduate School of Management. The amazing growth of the program shows the interest in entrepreneurial education that students in all fields of learning yearn for. They understand the nature and potential of starting an entrepreneurial business. I suspect many will get personally involved in a new venture not long after graduation.

I have visited many classes at UTD and at other local universities' management schools. The students taking entrepreneurial courses range widely in age and experience. Some are existing students, some fresh college graduates, and some are somewhat seasoned businesspeople. A few are successful entrepreneurs, but mostly in the early stages of their business life. The combination of students is interesting because it says that people are eager to learn how to start a business at any stage of their life. Entrepreneurism is probably the least understood aspect of business management education. Professor Joseph Picken is making a big difference in that calculus. His program has gained national attention and won several national awards. I have been privileged to be a small part of his effort.

For many entrepreneurs, advanced education is a luxury they can't afford. Still, there are many texts available for studying and developing the skills that are required to run a business. A rudimentary understanding of accounting and business law is essential. The biggest missing element for many would-be entrepreneurs is the enthusiasm and optimism that is absolutely required for success. That is not found in a classroom or in any book. If you don't have the burning desire, you probably won't find it in a book and you should probably seek a job, not start a business.

But before you give up and start hunting a job-job, I want you to reconsider all of the benefits of being an entrepreneur: potential wealth, calendar freedom and the ability to spend your leisure as you like without showing up on the front page of the newspaper. One of the most fundamental benefits that accrue to the entrepreneur is the ability to make quick decisions whether in business, charitable giving or recreation. Entrepreneurs can make a decision right now and write a check.

Entrepreneurs can make a decision right now and write a check. I would like to think that most successful entrepreneurs will share their success with their employees, with those in need and with other, less-seasoned beginning entrepreneurs. That means the entrepreneur should be sensitive to the many different needs of his community.

If you are a corporate officer, you must deal with upper management, a committee, and eventually the board of directors in order to make even a small donation. Relatively rare is the corporation that makes a large donation to a nonprofit when there no is no direct benefit to the corporation. As an entrepreneur, the timing and size of your donation is limited only by your own resources and inclinations. This is perhaps one of the greatest fringe benefits of succeeding at starting something.

By the way, a corporate officer will be of little help in giving you advice on starting a business. If they he anything about being an entrepreneur, he would probably not be a corporate officer but he would be a business owner!

The entrepreneurial lifestyle yields many benefits, but few are greater than the freedom to set one's own calendar and priorities. So, go start something!

CONTRACTS

In any business, large or small, contracts are a continuing issue to be dealt with. Careful attention is required to get it right. Do not be afraid to seek professional help well before you enter into a new contract, regardless of its nature.

First, a disclaimer: I am not a lawyer and I've had no legal training. All of my opinions on contracts and agreements are based on my own personal business experience and, therefore, might be technically inaccurate. Nevertheless, I think you can benefit from my experience. Warning: Before you enter into any significant contract or if you find yourself the target of a lawsuit, I urge you to acquire the services of a seasoned lawyer who has experience in your field.

Contracts and agreements are essential elements of any business, including entrepreneurial businesses. Unfortunately, poorly drawn contracts and agreements may become the central problem in an entrepreneurial business. Contracts done poorly will almost certainly result in financial and perhaps psychological disaster. Any legally enforceable contract should have the benefit of a careful study by you and your lawyer before it is executed. This includes any buy/sell arrangement between the partners. Of course, as I argued earlier, I would strongly discourage you from partnerships of any kind. *Be the owner or be the employee!*

Every single word and paragraph of a contract is important, and sometimes the importance will only become apparent when there is a dispute. You should never sign any contract that you have not reviewed personally and sought the assistance of a competent attorney to review on your behalf looking for items that will snag you later. There are many "poison pills" that can be inserted in a contract and may be almost unrecognizable to the untrained eye, potentially creating future problem for the entrepreneur.

I always recommend to any business person, especially entrepreneurs, that they insist that all contracts include an arbitration clause. The **American Arbitration Association** will provide you the language that should be inserted in your contract if your contract is to be subject to the AAA arbitration process. Your company lawyer may not feel the need for an arbitration clause; many do not. They may prefer to depend on the court system to settle arguments. *Overrule your lawyer! You absolutely want an arbitration clause in every contract you sign.*

You have probably heard of mediation in relation to contract law, and your lawyer may point to that as a better approach to contract settlements. But, mediation only occurs after a lawsuit has been filed. At that point your legal costs of dealing with a lawsuit can skyrocket and be almost limitless. However, mediation will occasionally work and if so, successfully shortcuts the legal process. Many judges now insist that the parties to a lawsuit go through mediation before they will accept the case in court for formal trial.

But the arbitration process is a much better way! If the language for arbitration is accurately included in the initial contract, it will guarantee a relatively quick and inexpensive resolution to any conflict. The most favorable aspect of arbitration, in my opinion, is that the arbitrators, the people who decide the case, are people who are familiar with the industry or issues involved. In small cases, there will be one arbitrator selected by the arbitration board.

In larger cases, each party gets to select an arbitrator from the arbitration panel and those two arbitrators select a third member from the panel. In either case, you will be provided with the full details on the arbitrators' backgrounds.

The decision of the arbitrators in an arbitration case is final. There will be no lawsuit or court trial after arbitration. The relevant court will enter the arbitrators' decision as an accomplished judgment of law. Any financial judgment rendered has the equal force of, and may have the same effect as, a court judgment. I would urge you to do a bit of research into the issue of arbitration versus lawsuit for settlement of contract disputes.

I strongly recommend that you always have an arbitration clause in all of your contracts.

The two parties to arbitration may represent themselves without lawyers, or one or both parties may be represented by attorneys. Attorneys are not required. Arbitration hearings are relatively informal and deal with the facts and the equity of the case. Case preparation can be similarly informal. The primary purpose of the brief presented to the arbitrators well before the arbitration is to inform relatively knowledgeable members of the panel of the relevant facts and circumstances of the argument. Since the arbitrators usually have experience in the field involved, your explanations will likely be well understood. In small cases, the entire arbitration might be done by mail and be completed in a matter of weeks.

In contrast to arbitration, in the normal court trial setting, a jury of six or twelve individuals may have zero knowledge of anything even slightly technical in your presentation. The trial itself might be delayed several months, or even years, depending on the availability of a court willing to take the case. It might also be delayed by strategic filings by one of the parties. The trial may become a lawyer popularity contest for the jury. The actual facts may not be all that relevant to the jury's decision if the opposing lawyer is very good with his presentations. Even if the parties agree to a trial by the judge with no jury, the odds that your judge will understand anything remotely technical can be pretty low.

A few years ago, I served as an arbitrator for the National Association of Securities Dealers (NASD) arbitration panel. I found the process of arbitration to be very straightforward and fundamentally fair. In all the cases that I decided, I had full understanding of all the technical issues as well as the legal issues. I felt very confident that my judgments were right on the money. I'm very sensitive to honesty in business, and regrettably, many lawsuits are brought by people who are less than honest. Your job is to give crafty people the smallest opportunity possible to attack you. And if they do attack you, you want the best method to defend yourself. I consider that to be the American Arbitration Association approach. In a court of law, frivolous lawsuits might find a setting to play out in. In arbitration, frivolous charges fail quickly. It's hard to fool a knowledgeable arbitrator.

In a typical lawsuit, the defendant sometimes loses even if he prevails in court. Because of the cost of the lawyers, the lost time and the emotional overload, a lawsuit can ruin your business, your marriage, your family, and forever destroy your peace of mind.

Throughout my career of 40 years in management I have filed only one lawsuit and that was in a investment situation unrelated to my business. I have never been sued. If someone had a grievance with our company, my staff and I made every effort to resolve it immediately. We tried to take all the emotion out of it, whether we were right or wrong, reduced the issue to dollars and cents, and then tried to work out a negotiated settlement. We succeeded every time. In my opinion, that's the best way to handle conflict. The largest bonus from all of this was that we retained customers and suppliers and created no enemies. A few times, we might have given up a few more dollars than would have been lost in a lawsuit, but we saved 10 times that amount in avoiding the other legal and soft costs and the emotional grief that goes with a lawsuit.

I always considered it a gigantic bargain when an issue was settled quickly! Almost always, the early settlement was the best bet financially and emotionally. Don't let your pride get involved. Never sue based on principle. Sue only for money; that's the only good motive for a lawsuit. In order to justify a full-blown lawsuit the dollar numbers need to be big. Legal costs can go through the ceiling and strip you of all your invested resources even if you win.

Enter into contracts the way you would go into the deepest jungle, very carefully and completely aware of the strange beasties that inhabit the tall grass and deep forest around you. Be sure to insist on an arbitration clause in all of your contracts. And, don't be afraid to seek professional help from an attorney at the outset.

PRICING

The manner in which you set the pricing for your products or services will largely determine your profitability. A 1% change in price can mean a 20% change in profit. You, as the owner, are solely responsible for the profitability of your company and you must take charge of all pricing decisions. Don't rely on a sales department or an individual sales manager or salesman to set prices for your products. They can advise you, but remember that the final decision is yours alone!

A number of years ago I was approached by a friend, an entrepreneur of business owner, who had been running his business in absentia. He had turned the company's day-to-day operations over to a subordinate who was fresh out of an executive position in a very large corporation. My friend moved to France and expected to collect nice dividends from his business. After a couple of years, the business was losing money and was in danger of going broke. He returned from France and asked me if I would visit with him and give him some ideas on what to do. I asked him to bring along his longtime financial officer and meet me for lunch at a local restaurant. I brought my executive vice-president so that we could have a broad, four-party discussion.

My friend, the CEO and owner, had just fired the general manager and taken responsibility for running the business himself. After we listened to his explanation of where the company was from a profit and loss (P&L) standpoint, he complained that the company was enmeshed in some very lossy long-term contracts.

I began to ask him a few questions, the first one being, "Who in the company establishes pricing?" He said, "Why, the sales department, who else?" At that point, I knew the solution to his problems, with no more information needed. In a small company, the only person who can set and approve final pricing for contracts and products or services is the CEO/owner. A sales manager's job is to get orders and not necessarily to maintain profits. The CEO simply cannot depend on the sales department to maintain healthy margins. The recently departed general manager was himself a salesman and seemingly had little regard for profitability. I'm not sure he even completely understood the impact of pricing decisions on profitability.

After listening to all their information on the company's present status, we suggested that he take two steps: first, as CEO, take over all pricing decisions; and second, call his customers and ask for a price increase in mid-contract. He should explain that without a price increase he feared bankruptcy, potentially resulting in the company's failure to deliver critical products. The company manufactured components for military electronic systems, so a shutdown would be a big issue.

He felt that trying to renegotiate pricing in the middle of an ongoing contract would be considered a bad business practice and that none of his customers would agree to it. We informed him that, contrary to his opinion, we had succeeded several times in doing just that. In our case the problem was related to wild variations in the value of the Japanese yen versus the US dollar. As importers, we were very dependent on currency exchange rates. Most of our products were coming from Japan, some from Taiwan. No customer likes a price increase, but sometimes there's no viable alternative. We told him that it was something to try, and that some customers would reluctantly agree and some might fight him. But, if you can convince just 50% of your customers to accept a price increase, you've made a vast improvement. He actually did achieve a bit better than 50% in renegotiating favorable contract price modifications. As a bonus, he lost no customers in the process.

He agreed that as CEO, he would take personal responsibility for all future pricing decisions! The sales department should suggest prices and recommend pricing policy, but they should have no responsibility for the final pricing decision. He became the court of last resort for pricing, just as it should be in any successful small company. As the owner and CEO, you should review every pricing decision. He did exactly that from that point forward!

Two months later, his company was profitable, and the company has been profitable ever since. The most basic rule in an entrepreneurial business is that the CEO/owner is ultimately responsible for profit and loss. If you lose money it should be your fault, not that of one of your subordinates. The buck and the bottom line stops with you. No excuses!

I had another experience that greatly modified my thinking on pricing. I attended a Young Presidents Organization (YPO) "University" in the late 1970s. I hosted one of the conference speakers, who was a pricing specialist and consultant. I had no idea what to expect from him, but my job was to set up the room and all of the various things he needed to do his talk: a microphone and speaker system, a large marker board and a podium. That was the total extent of my effort except for introducing him to a crowd of about 250 company presidents, most of them entrepreneurs and owners of their own businesses. By the way, the YPO universities are incredible learning opportunities; try your best to secure membership in YPO.

The "resource", as YPO speakers are referred to, started his lecture by writing on the easel with a big black marker his proposed approach to setting price on a new product. He jotted down material, labor, and factory overhead; then summed that up and added a figure for general administrative and marketing costs. He then calculated the total cost, looked out at the crowd, and said, "Now we need to add a fair profit"—a slight pause—"how about 10%, that's a fair profit, isn't it?" Most of the 200+ attendees nodded in agreement and he did just that, added 10% and underlined the result. He beamed at the crowd and announced, "This is the way we set pricing!" Again, there was some nodding agreement.

He paused a second, looked around the room and then shouted, "What a bunch of idiots! Surely you're not CEOs!"

He continued, "*That's not the way you set prices*! Prices are set by the market, not by the cost of the product. The only reason for cost analysis is to determine whether or not you can play in the market."

In other words, he said the cost is, many, times irrelevant to pricing.

He followed up with a rhetorical question: "What constitutes a fair profit?" Without waiting for any replies, he answered that a fair profit is that profit (or loss) that results from a free exchange between a buyer and a seller. That is the essence of Adam Smith's "invisible hand" approach to free-market enterprise. If you overcharge for your product, perhaps no one will buy it or a competitor will undercut your price.

The speaker then held up a Cross pen and a Bic ballpoint pen as an example of two products that are functionally interchangeable yet have wide differences in pricing. He turned his back to the audience and did a bit of writing on a white tablet with each of the two pens. Then he defied anyone to tell him which pen had done which writing. Functional equivalence! Yet the Cross pen's price is in the neighborhood of $30, while the Bic pen sells for about 1% of that, under $0.30. In fact, refills for the Cross pen cost from three to five times the price of a Bic pen. Check it out at Wal-Mart!

He then asked, "How can Cross sell their pen for $30 when it is functionally equivalent to a pen selling for so much less?" The answer is simple: Buyers buy pens in a free market exchange. No one forces them to buy or merchants to sell. A better answer is that Cross chooses to sell their elegant product into the high-end gift market while Bic serves the basic functional pen market.

No one would consider presenting a Bic pen as a gift. That would be a nasty insult. If a Cross pen is presented, that gift shows respect. The Cross people know their market and the market sets the price. The control on overpricing is free competition. If you overprice, your competitors will cut you to pieces. Market-pricing discipline is always at work. As an entrepreneur, you will live or die by it. It will never be easy. But never give up!

Be careful on price setting. A seemingly minor 1% price cut may mean a 10 to 20% profit cut. Remember that cost and selling price are not necessarily related. You may be wooed by your salesmen to give up a few percent on price in order to lock up a quick sale. Don't do it! First, check how much effect that price cut has on profitability. Remember, salesmen are rarely responsible for the P&L, you are! Sometimes you have to face down the customer on pricing, with the realization that you might lose the sale. It'd better to lose unprofitable business!

<u>You</u> are the bottom line on the P&L!

CONCLUSION

Every idea in this book is a result of my personal entrepreneurial experiences over the last 50 years in business and my observations of many successful and unsuccessful entrepreneurs. I hope that you have profited from reading it. No one can guarantee your success, only you can make that happen. Success is usually the result of good thinking, hard work and a bit of luck. It always helps if you can catch a good wave. Your surfboard ride to the beach will be a lot more satisfying if you have picked the right wave. It doesn't have to be the best wave, but just good enough to get you up on your surfboard and headed for the beach.

Your energy and your endurance will be taxed in any business start-up. You can expect that. Starting a business is extraordinarily hard work with little time for play at the outset, but the incredible rewards of your success will be amazing. Once you experience some measure of success in your own business, you will never go back to a job. Rare is the successful entrepreneur who ever thinks of leaving his business and trying to go back to a job. Quitting the entrepreneurial world would mean being required to report to somebody else. Once someone has tasted the joy of entrepreneurial activity, they can rarely accept not being in charge of their own destiny.

You cannot avoid risk in life; it's always there, right beside you, but as an entrepreneur you will think that it has gone on steroids. To some extent, that's part of the fun. It certainly can add adrenaline to an otherwise dull existence. Several people have described flying combat jets as hours and hours of boredom interrupted occasionally by a few seconds of stark terror. Running an entrepreneurial business of your own is a lot like that. In both of these activities you are truly living on the edge!

The entrepreneurial experience is one that you will treasure for the rest of your life. Even if you fail, you will probably learn enough to try again. Failure in a business start-up is not the end of the world. It may just make you stronger. There is nothing like life on the edge!

But always remember to pack your parachute. You might need it if things go poorly. You would always like to live to fight another day. I have great confidence that you can survive the life of the entrepreneur, life on the edge!

One of the most incredible icons of the modern world, Winston Churchill, said it best during England's darkest hours in World War II:

"Never, never, never, never give up."

Any successful entrepreneur will tell you that your persistence in the face of seemingly overwhelming odds will be your measure of success. Never give up! No matter how dark it gets, slog on! Your eventual victory will make it all worthwhile.

Enjoy life on the edge . . .

Get out there and <u>Go start something!</u>

ACKNOWLEDGMENTS

Over the last several years that I have worked on this book of rules, I have had a lot of feedback from students and professors at the various business schools around the Dallas area. Special thanks go to Joe Picken and Jim Gibbons, both of whom are responsible for management education in the Dallas and Fort Worth Metroplex, with Joe being a specialist in entrepreneurship. I had encouragement from Eileen Resnik, head of the North Texas University Murphy Center for Entrepreneurship.

I received considerable editorial assistance from my dear wife, Suzanne; my daughters, Kathryn, Sheryl and Deborah; and my sister-in-law, Judy Collmer, PhD. I owe special thanks to my daughter Kathryn who went above and beyond the call of duty to finalize the edit.

This is the first book that I have undertaken and I received support from many other people encouraging me to complete it. I hope that it serves you well as you move toward an entrepreneurial experience.